EXTRA DRILLS & PRACTICES

WILLARD D. SHEELER

This book is co-distributed in the United States of America by English Language Services, Inc. and Oxford University Press, Inc.

ENGLISH LANGUAGE SERVICES, INC.

Published by English Language Services, Inc.

Copyright © English Language Services, Inc. 1978
Philippines Copyright 1978
Taiwan Copyright 1978
Indonesia Copyright 1978
Korea Copyright 1978

Library of Congress Catalog Card Number 75-10596

All rights reserved. No part of this book may be reproduced or transmitted in any form or by any means, electronic or mechanical, including photocopying, recording or by any information storage and retrieval system, without permission in advance in writing from the publisher, English Language Services, Inc.

Printing   2   3   4   5   6   7   8   9   10

ISBN 0-89285-039-6

Printed in the United States of America

INTRODUCTION

The two hundred drills and practices in *Extra Drills and Practices* are organized around sixty-eight grammatical points. The numbered points are represented by the large numbers you see in the Table of Contents and in the body of this drillbook. These numbers correspond to those used for the grammar points in *Grammar and Drillbook*.

This drillbook can be used for class practice or for home study. All drills have only one answer, or can be 'worked' in only one way. A key, printed in the back of the book, is provided for many of the drills. A few drills are not completed in the textbook, but are left for the teacher to complete. Questions for these drills are included in the key.

A variety of drill formats is used; repetition, build-ups, substitution, cued reply, transformation, combination, expansion, fixed reply and restatement. Many of the drills are of the Speaker A/Speaker B type. In these, two learners each take a different role and they speak and reply according to a 'statement of fact' of provided information.

This drillbook forms part of a correlated program, but it can also be used independently—in class or at home—to supplement other basic course materials on an intermediate or high intermediate level. When used independently, a preview of the vocabulary used in the drills will be helpful so that students do not encounter a heavy load of new vocabulary while trying to concentrate on the drill proper.

As part of a correlated program, *Extra Drills and Practices* supplements Books 5 and 6 of the *Welcome to English* series and the *Grammar and Drillbook*. The two basic textbooks illustrate the grammar in context—in dialogs, readings and conversations—and also give some drill and exercise practice. The *Grammar and Drillbook* explains the grammar in narrative form and gives extensive exercise practice. The books may be used singly, or in any combination.

TABLE OF CONTENTS

NOUN PHRASES — 1-39

1 Nouns — 1-3
Extra Drill 1.1: Plural Forms of Regular Nouns [1]
Extra Drill 1.2: Plural Forms of Regular Nouns [2]
Extra Drill 1.3: Plural Forms of Irregular Nouns [3]

2 Count Nouns and Mass Nouns — 3-9
Extra Drill 2.1: Count Nouns (Stress with Numbers and *a*) [3]
Extra Drill 2.2: Count Nouns (Fruits and Vegetables) [4]
Extra Drill 2.3: Mass Nouns [4]
Extra Drill 2.4: Mass Nouns (Stress with *some* and *the*) [5]
Extra Drill 2.5: *A* with Count Nouns; *some* with Mass Nouns [5]
Extra Drill 2.6: *Some* with Count and Mass Nouns [7]
Extra Drill 2.7: Containers and Measures (Stress of *of*) [7]
Extra Drill 2.8: Nouns in a Series (Intonation) [8]

3 Words Used as Both Count and Mass Nouns — 9-10
Extra Drill 3.1: Words Used as Both Count and Mass Nouns [9]
Extra Drill 3.2: Countable Uses of Some Mass Nouns [10]

4 Some Noun Modifiers — 11-13
Extra Drill 4.1: Adjectives as Noun Modifiers (Stress) [11]
Extra Drill 4.2: Premodifying Nouns (Stress) [11]
Extra Drill 4.3: Premodifying Nouns [12]
Extra Drill 4.4: Noun Possessives as Noun Modifiers [13]

5 Noun Determiners — 13
Extra Drill 5.1: Noun Determiners (Introductory) [13]

6 Articles and Demonstratives; *some, any, no* — 14-17
Extra Drill 6.1: Noun Determiners *a* (or *an*) and *the* [14]
Extra Drill 6.2: Noun Determiners *some* and *any* with Plural [14]
Extra Drill 6.3: Noun Determiners *some* and *any* with Plural and Mass Nouns [15]
Extra Drill 6.4: Noun Determiners *some* and *any* in Questions [16]
Extra Drill 6.5: Noun Determiners *no* and *not...any* [17]

8 Noun Modifiers: Prepositional Phrases — 18-19
Extra Drill 8.1: Prepositional Phrases as Noun Modifiers [18]
Extra Drill 8.2: Prepositional Phrases as Noun Modifiers [18]
Extra Drill 8.3: Prepositional Phrases as Noun Modifiers [19]

9 Pronouns — 19-20
Extra Drill 9.1: Subject and Object Pronouns [19]
Extra Drill 9.2: Subject and Object Pronouns [20]

10 Noun Determiners: *more* and *most; enough; plenty of* — 21
Extra Drill 10.1: Noun Determiner *enough* [21]
Extra Drill 10.2: Noun Determiner *enough* [21]

11 Noun Determiners: *a lot of* and *lots of; much/many; a little/a few; a great (good) deal of* — 22-24
Extra Drill 11.1: Noun Determiners: *a lot of* and *lots of* [22]
Extra Drill 11.2: Noun Determiners: *many* and *much* [23]
Extra Drill 11.3: Noun Determiners: *little* and *few* [23]

12 Noun Substitutes — 24-26
Extra Drill 12.1: Noun Substitutes *many, much, a little, a few* [24]
Extra Drill 12.2: Noun Substitutes (Quantity, Demonstratives) [25]
Extra Drill 12.3: Noun Substitutes (Possessive Pronouns) [26]

14 Adjective Precedence — 26-28
Extra Drill 14.1: Adjective Precedence (Stress) [26]
Extra Drill 14.2: Adjective Precedence [27]
Extra Drill 14.3: Adjective Precedence [28]

15 Noun Determiners *some* and *any* with Strong Stress — 28-29
Extra Drill 15.1: Noun Determiners *some* and *any* with Strong Stress [28]

16 Noun Determiners: *either/neither; another/other; each* **and** *every* — 29-31
    Extra Drill 16.1: Noun Determiners *either* and *neither* [29]
    Extra Drill 16.2: Noun Substitutes *another* and *others* [30]
    Extra Drill 16.3: Noun Substitutes *the other* and *the others* [30]
    Extra Drill 16.4: Noun Determiners *every* and *each* [31]
    Extra Drill 16.5: Noun Determiners Before *one* (Stress) [31]

17 Indefinite Pronouns — 32-35
    Extra Drill 17.1: Indefinite Pronouns (Stress) [32]
    Extra Drill 17.2: Indefinite Pronouns *some-, any-, no-* [32]
    Extra Drill 17.3: Possessive Indefinite Pronouns [33]
    Extra Drill 17.4: Possessive Indefinite *somebody else's* [33]
    Extra Drill 17.5: Indefinite Pronouns Modified by Adjectives [34]
    Extra Drill 17.6: Indefinite Pronouns Modified by Prepositional Phrases [35]

19 Noun Determiners: *all (the)* **and** *both (the)* — 35-36
    Extra Drill 19.1: Noun Determiner *all (the)* [35]
    Extra Drill 19.2: *They all* and *they both* [36]

20 Predeterminers — 37-38
    Extra Drill 20.1: Predeterminer *each* [37]
    Extra Drill 20.2: Predeterminer *every one* [38]
    Extra Drill 20.3: Predeterminers [38]

21 Adjective + *one* **or** *ones* — 39
    Extra Drill 21.1: Adjective + *one(s)* (Stress) [39]

22 Pre-Noun Modifiers (Summary) — 39
    Extra Drill 22.1: Order of Pre-Noun Modifiers [39]

DIRECT AND INDIRECT SPEECH — 39-65

24 Sentences as Objects of Transitive Verbs — 39-40
    Extra Drill 24.1: Sentence as Object of *say* [39]

25 Direct Speech — 40
    Extra Drill 25.1: Direct Speech Quotations [40]

26 Indirect Speech — 40-41
    Extra Drill 26.1: Indirect Speech [40]

27 Indirect Speech: Verb Forms and Tenses — 41-44
    Extra Drill 27.1: Past Tense in Indirect Speech [41]
    Extra Drill 27.2: Past Modals in Indirect Speech [42]
    Extra Drill 27.3: Past Modals in Indirect Speech [43]
    Extra Drill 27.4: Past Perfect in Indirect Speech [44]

28 Indirect Speech: Choice of Tenses — 45-46
    Extra Drill 28.1: Present Tense after *said* in Indirect Speech [45]
    Extra Drill 28.2: Present Perfect after *said* in Indirect Speech [46]

29 *Wh-* Question Words — 47-49
    Extra Drill 29.1: Question Words *which* and *whose* + NP [47]
    Extra Drill 29.2: Question Words *who, what, when, where, why, how* [48]
    Extra Drill 29.3: Question Word *how* + Adjective [49]

30 Indirect Questions: *Wh-* **Questions** — 50-54
    Extra Drill 30.1: Indirect *Wh-* Questions [50]
    Extra Drill 30.2: Indirect *Wh-* Questions [50]
    Extra Drill 30.3: Indirect *Wh-* Questions [51]
    Extra Drill 30.4: Indirect *Wh-* Questions [52]
    Extra Drill 30.5: Indirect *Wh-* Questions [53]
    Extra Drill 30.6: Included *Wh-* Questions (After "I don't know") [54]
    Extra Drill 30.7: Included *Wh-* Questions [54]

31 Indirect Questions: Yes/No Questions — 55-58
    Extra Drill 31.1: Indirect Yes/No Questions with *if* [55]
    Extra Drill 31.2: Indirect Yes/No Questions with *if* [55]
    Extra Drill 31.3: Indirect Yes/No Questions with *if* [56]
    Extra Drill 31.4: Indirect Yes/No Questions with *whether...or not* [57]
    Extra Drill 31.5: Included Yes/No Questions with *whether...or not* [57]
    Extra Drill 31.6: Included Yes/No Questions with *if...or not* [58]

32 Indirect Speech: with Imperatives   58-60
    Extra Drill 32.1: Imperatives in Indirect Speech [58]
    Extra Drill 32.2: Imperatives in Indirect Speech (Negative) [59]
    Extra Drill 32.3: Imperatives in Indirect Speech [59]

33 Indirect Speech: Pronoun Forms   60-61
    Extra Drill 33.1: Pronouns in Indirect Speech [60]
    Extra Drill 33.2: Pronouns in Indirect Speech [61]

34 Indirect Speech: Adverbials of Time and Place; Verbs *come/go* and *bring/take*   62-65
    Extra Drill 34.1: *Here* and *there* in Indirect Speech [62]
    Extra Drill 34.2: Time Adverbials in Indirect Speech [62]
    Extra Drill 34.3: Time Adverbials in Indirect Speech [63]
    Extra Drill 34.4: Summary Drill: Reporting Speech [65]

INFINITIVES AND GERUNDS; CONJUNCTIONS AND COMPOUNDING   66-96

35 Verb + Infinitive   66-67
    Extra Drill 35.1: Verb + Infinitive [66]
    Extra Drill 35.2: Verb + Infinitive [66]
    Extra Drill 35.3: Verb + Infinitive [67]
    Extra Drill 35.4: Verb + Infinitive [67]

36 Special Verb Expressions   68-70
    Extra Drill 36.1: Verb Expression *be to* [68]
    Extra Drill 36.2: Verb Expression *be supposed to* [68]
    Extra Drill 36.3: Verb Expressions *have to, used to, be about to* [69]
    Extra Drill 36.4: Special Verb Expressions (with Indirect Speech) [70]

37 Adjective + Infinitive   71
    Extra Drill 37.1: Adjective + Infinitive [71]

38 Verb or Adjective + Infinitive: Short Answers   71-73
    Extra Drill 38.: Short Answers to Verb + Infinitive [71]
    Extra Drill 38.2: Short Answers to Verb or Adjective + Infinitive [72]
    Extra Drill 38.3: Negative Short Answers to Verb or Adjective + Infinitive [72]

39 Infinitive of Purpose   73
    Extra Drill 39.1: Infinitive of Purpose [73]

40 Verb + Gerund   74
    Extra Drill 40.1: Verb + Gerund [74]

41 Preposition + Gerund   75-77
    Extra Drill 41.1: Verb or Preposition + Gerund [75]
    Extra Drill 41.2: Verb or Preposition + Gerund [76]
    Extra Drill 41.3: Short Answers to Verb or Preposition + Gerund [77]
    Extra Drill 41.4: *It* as Substitute for a Gerund [77]

42 Verbs Followed by Either Gerunds or Infinitives   78
    Extra Drill 42.1: Verb + Either Infinitive or Gerund [78]

43 Gerunds and Infinitives as Subjects and Complements   78-79
    Extra Drill 43.1: Gerunds as Complements of *be* [78]
    Extra Drill 43.2: Negative Gerund as Subject of Sentence [79]

44 *It* and *there* as Sentence Subjects   80-82
    Extra Drill 44.1: *It* as Subject; Infinitive in Complement [80]
    Extra Drill 44.2: Gerund as Subject [80]
    Extra Drill 44.3: *There* as Subject [81]
    Extra Drill 44.4: *There* as Subject; Gerund in Complement [82]

45 Nominal Phrases   83-86
    Extra Drill 45.1: Nominal Phrases (Stress) [83]
    Extra Drill 45.2: Adjective + Nominal Phrase (Stress) [83]
    Extra Drill 45.3: Nominal Phrases [83]
    Extra Drill 45.4: Nominal Phrases [84]
    Extra Drill 45.5: Nominal Phrases (without Sentence Stress) [85]
    Extra Drill 45.6: Adjective + Nominal Phrase (Stress) [85]
    Extra Drill 45.7: Nominal Phrases (with Contrast Stress) [85]

46 Noun Compounds — 86-89
Extra Drill 46.1: Noun Compounds (Stress) [86]
Extra Drill 46.2: Noun Compounds Having Gerunds (Stress) [86]
Extra Drill 46.3: Noun Compounds Having Gerunds (Stress) [87]
Extra Drill 46.4: Noun Compounds (without Sentence Stress) [87]
Extra Drill 46.5: Noun Compounds (without Sentence Stress) [88]
Extra Drill 46.6: Noun Compounds [88]

47 Compound Noun Phrases — 89-93
Extra Drill 47.1: Compound Noun Phrases with *and* [89]
Extra Drill 47.2: Compound Noun Phrases with *and* [89]
Extra Drill 47.3: Compound Noun Phrases with *or* [90]
Extra Drill 47.4: Noun Phrases with *or* in Alternative Questions [91]
Extra Drill 47.5: Noun Phrases with *or* in Unlimited Choice [91]
Extra Drill 47.6: Compound Noun Phrases with More Than Two Items [92]
Extra Drill 47.7: *Both...and* in Compound Noun Phrases [92]

48 Conjunctions with Other Structures — 93
Extra Drill 48.1: Practices Joined with *and* [93]

49 The Conjunction *but* — 94-95
Extra Drill 49.1: Noun Phrases Joined with *but* (Stress) [94]
Extra Drill 49.2: Noun Phrases Joined with *but* [94]
Extra Drill 49.3: Conjunctions with *but* [95]

50 Special Nouns in Reference to Number — 95-96
Extra Drill 50.1: Special Nouns [95]

APPOSITIVES, PARTICIPLES; INDIRECT OBJECTS AND OTHER COMPLEMENT CONSTRUCTIONS — 96-131

51 Adjectives Used as Nominals — 96
Extra Drill 51.1: Adjectives Used as Nominals [96]

52 Appositives — 97-99
Extra Drill 52.1: Appositives [97]
Extra Drill 52.2: Appositives (Intonation) [97]
Extra Drill 52.3: Appositives [98]
Extra Drill 52.4: Appositives (with No Pause) [98]
Extra Drill 52.5: Appositives [99]

53 Infinitives and Gerunds with Different Meanings after Certain Verbs — 99-101
Extra Drill 53.1: *Stop* + Infinitive of Purpose [99]
Extra Drill 53.2: *Stop* + Gerund [100]
Extra Drill 53.3: *Remember* + Infinitive [100]
Extra Drill 53.4: *Remember* + Gerund [101]

54 Compound Modifiers Using Numbers — 102-103
Extra Drill 54.1: Stress of Compound Modifiers Using Numbers [102]
Extra Drill 54.2: Compound Modifiers Using Numbers [103]

55 Noun Phrase + Infinitive — 103-105
Extra Drill 55.1: Noun Phrase (Gerund) + Infinitive Modifier [103]
Extra Drill 55.2: Noun Phrase + Infinitive Modifier [104]
Extra Drill 55.3: Noun Phrase + Infinitive Modifier [105]
Extra Drill 55.4: Noun Phrase + Infinitive Modifier [105]

56 Participles as Noun Modifiers: *-ing* Form — 106-109
Extra Drill 56.1: *-ing* Participles as Noun Modifiers [106]
Extra Drill 56.2: *-ing* Participles as Noun Modifiers [106]
Extra Drill 56.3: Contrasting Stress with *-ing* Modifiers [107]
Extra Drill 56.4: *-ing* Participle Phrase as Noun Modifier [107]
Extra Drill 56.5: *-ing* Participle Modifiers without Object or Complement [108]
Extra Drill 56.6: *-ing* Participle Modifier—From a Simple Present Verb Form [109]

57 *-ing* Forms as True Adjectives — 109
Extra Drill 57.1: *-ing* Participles as True Adjectives [109]

58 Participles as Noun Modifiers: *-ed* Form   110–114
    Extra Drill 58.1: *-ed* Participle as Noun Modifier [110]
    Extra Drill 58.2: *-ed* Participle as Noun Modifier [110]
    Extra Drill 58.3: *-ed* Participle Phrase as Modifier of Noun [111]
    Extra Drill 58.4: *-ed* Participle Phrase as Modifier of Noun [112]
    Extra Drill 58.5: Negative *-ed* Participle Phrase as Modifier of Noun [112]
    Extra Drill 58.6: *-ed* Participles and Participle Phrases as Noun Modifiers [113]
    Extra Drill 58.7: *-ed* Participle as Noun Modifier [113]
    Extra Drill 58.8: *-ed* Participle as Noun Modifier [114]

59 Contrast of *-ing* and *-ed* Forms   115
    Extra Drill 59.1: Contrast of *-ing* and *-ed* Participle Modifiers [115]

60 Verbs Followed by Two Objects: Indirect Object with *to*   116–120
    Extra Drill 60.1: Indirect Object with *to* (Noun Form) [116]
    Extra Drill 60.2: Indirect Object without a Preposition [116]
    Extra Drill 60.3: Indirect Object with *to* (Pronoun Form) [117]
    Extra Drill 60.4: Pronoun Forms of Both Direct and Indirect Objects [117]
    Extra Drill 60.5: Pronoun Form of Indirect Object (with Stress Contrast) [118]
    Extra Drill 60.6: Pronoun Form of Indirect Object (Stress Contrast on Sentence Subject) [118]
    Extra Drill 60.7: Pronoun Form of Indirect Object (with Stress Contrast) [119]
    Extra Drill 60.8: Direct and Indirect Object (without Preposition) [120]

61 Verbs Followed by Two Objects: Indirect Object with *for*   120–122
    Extra Drill 61.1: Direct and Indirect Object with *for* [120]
    Extra Drill 61.2: Indirect Object with *for* [121]
    Extra Drill 61.3: Indirect Object with *to* and *for* [122]

62 Verbs Followed by Two Objects: Fixed Order   123
    Extra Drill 62.1: Indirect Object with *to* or *for* [123]

63 Verbs Followed by an Infinitive with Subject   123–127
    Extra Drill 63.1: Verb Followed by an Infinitive with Subject [123]
    Extra Drill 63.2: Verb Followed by an Infinitive with Subject [124]
    Extra Drill 63.3: Verb Followed by an Infinitive with Subject [124]
    Extra Drill 63.4: Verb Followed by an Infinitive with Subject [125]
    Extra Drill 63.5: Verb Followed by Infinitive Particle *to* with Subject [125]
    Extra Drill 63.6: Verb Followed by a Negative Infinitive with Subject [126]
    Extra Drill 63.7: Negative Verb Followed by Infinitive with Subject [126]

64 Verbs Followed by a Base Form with Subject   127–128
    Extra Drill 64.1: Verb Followed by a Base Form with Subject [127]
    Extra Drill 64.2: Verb Followed by a Base Form with Subject [127]

65 Verbs Followed by a Gerund with Subject   128–129
    Extra Drill 65.1: Verb Followed by a Gerund with Subject [128]
    Extra Drill 65.2: Verb Followed by a Gerund with Subject [128]
    Extra Drill 65.3: Verb Followed by a Gerund with Subject [129]

66 Verbs Followed by NP (Object) + NP (Complement)   129
    Extra Drill 66.1: Verb Object Followed by a Noun Phrase Complement [129]

67 Verbs Followed by NP (Object) + Adjective (Complement)   130–131
    Extra Drill 67.1: Verb Object Followed by an Adjective Complement [130]
    Extra Drill 67.2: Verb Object Followed by an Adjective Complement [130]

68 The Use of *for* + an Infinitive with Subject   131
    Extra Drill 68.1: Adjective Followed by an Infinitive with *for* + Subject [131]

1 NOUNS

Extra Drill 1.1 — Plural Forms of Regular Nouns

Repeat first the singular, then the plural form.

A. Nouns ending in a voiceless consonant /p, t, k, f, θ/ add /-s/

cup	boat	cake	cuff
shop	cat	cook	proof
map	carrot	desk	month
tape	coat	bike	birth

B. Nouns ending in a sibilant /s, z, š, ž, č, ǰ/ add /-iz/

bus	church	dish
class	lunch	brush
dress	speech	crash
price	sandwich	push
size	change	garage
noise	language	mirage
surprise	orange	
exercise	package	

C. Nouns ending in a voiced consonant or a vowel add /-z/

job	room	ball	boy
verb	farm	hotel	eye
friend	barn	chair	cow
ride	lesson	car	radio
egg	thing	stove	sea
rug	building	olive	lady

Extra Drill 1.2 | **Plural Forms of Regular Nouns**

Answer with the number *two* **and the plural form of the noun. Pay careful attention to the** /-s/, /-z/, **or** /-ɪz/ **plural ending sounds.**

1. Did you get a watch for your birthday?
   I got two watches.
2. Does he keep his money in a bank?
   He keeps it in two banks.
3. Was she reading a book about Canada?
   ....
4. Was there a spoiled banana?
   ....
5. Does she have a green blouse?
   ....
6. Did he drop a pea on the floor?
   ....
7. Do you have enough to fill a box?
   ....
8. Is there a circus in town?
   ....
9. Do they have a sofa like that on sale?
   ....
10. Did a camel die on the way?
    ....
11. Are they going to hire a nurse?
    ....
12. Did the teacher assign a page for tomorrow?
    ....
13. Did they break a cup?
    ....
14. Do we have to unlock a door to get in there?
    ....
15. Did you cook a pot of soup for them?
    ....

| Extra Drill 1.3 | **Plural Forms of Irregular Nouns** |

Take the part of Speaker B and answer according to the cued word. Use the number *two*.

SPEAKER A	SPEAKER B
1. Did they find the dogs? *(child)*	No, but they found two children.
2. Did Billy break his arm? *(tooth)*	No, but he broke two teeth.
3. Did you see a fireman? *(policeman)*	....
4. Did she buy a butter knife? *(steak knife)*	....
5. Did you eat the steak? *(fish)*	....
6. Did Mr. Lane lose a cow? *(calf)*	....
7. Did you see a man there? *(woman)*	....
8. Did she ask the manager? *(salesman)*	....
9. Did it kill a goose? *(sheep)*	....
10. Did Mrs. Finch bake a pie? *(loaf of bread)*	....
11. Did Felix catch a rat? *(mouse)*	....
12. Did Paul Martin play in an All-star Game? *(World Series)*	....
13. Did the wind damage any stores? *(house)*	....

2 COUNT NOUNS AND MASS NOUNS

| Extra Drill 2.1 | **Count Nouns (Stress with Numbers and *a*)** |

Substitute.

A. He's *an ártist*.
　　　a barber
　　　a dentist
　　　a doctor

B. Thrêe *vísitors* arrived.
　　　　customers
　　　　gentlemen
　　　　officers

C. I know *twô proféssors*.
　　　　six musicians
　　　　three mechanics
　　　　four policemen

Extra Drill 2.2 — Count Nouns (Fruits and Vegetables)

Change the sentences.

1. We can't grow banánas here.
   Bananas won't grów here.
2. They can't grow óranges there.
   Oranges won't grów there.
3. We can't grow peáches here.
   ....
4. We can't grow potátoes here.
   ....
5. They can't grow pineápples there.
   ....
6. We can't grow fígs here.
   ....
7. They can't grow grápes there.
   ....
8. We can't grow lémons here.
   ....
9. They can't grow cárrots there.
   ....
10. We can't grow papáyas here.
    ....

Extra Drill 2.3 — Mass Nouns

Substitute.

Food is quite expensive.
Meat
Cheese
Furniture
Clothing
Oil
Gas

| Extra Drill 2.4 | **Mass Nouns (Stress with *some* and *the*)** |

Substitute progressively.

	May I serve you sóme ríce?
some tea	May I serve you some tea?
some meat	. . . .
some corn	. . . .
Won't you have	. . . .
some cabbage	. . . .
some lettuce	. . . .
some coffee	. . . .
some chicken	. . . .
May I serve you	. . . .
some turkey	. . . .
Please pass	Please pass thé túrkey.
the butter	. . . .
the sugar	. . . .
the salt	. . . .
Would you like	. . . .
some soup	. . . .
some cream	. . . .
the bread	. . . .
the pepper	. . . .

| Extra Drill 2.5 | ***A* with Count Nouns; *some* with Mass Nouns** |

Each picture shows one mass noun and one count noun. Use the pictured nouns to substitute in the model sentence. Give the mass noun before the count noun.

He wants some water; he doesn't want a glass.

He wants some rice; he doesn't want a potato.

3.

4.

5.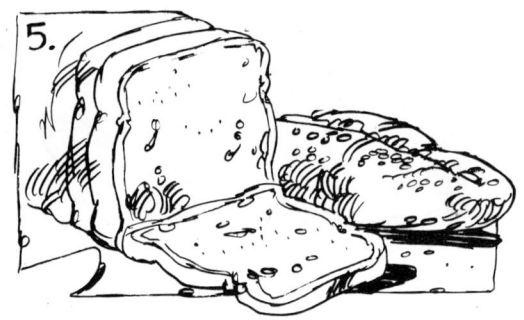

6.

7.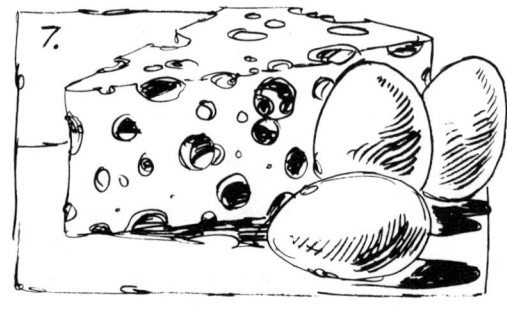

8.

9.

10.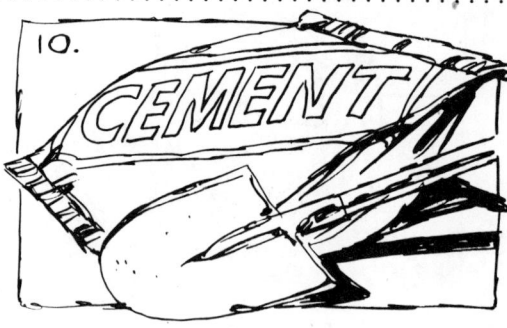

| Extra Drill 2.6 | *Some* with Count and Mass Nouns |

Substitute progressively.

	I wanted some coffee.
tea	I wanted some tea.
peach	....
need	....
money	....
fish	....
onion	....
buy	....
cheese	....
she	....
apple	....
coffee	....
milk	....
Yes/No Question	Did she buy some milk?

| Extra Drill 2.7 | Containers and Measures (Stress of *of*) |

In noun phrases such as *a bottle of milk* or *two bowls of soup* the word *of* is commonly pronounced /ə/.

A. **Listen and repeat.**

a glâss of mílk   twô pôunds of súgar
a bowl of soup   two heads of cabbage
a bar of soap   two pieces of paper

B. Look at the pictures and answer the questions with a container of measure of the mass nouns. Follow the model for Speaker B.

SPEAKER A: What did Mr. Ames have for breakfast?
SPEAKER B: A glass of orange juice, a piece of toast and a bowl of cereal.

What are you going to get at the drugstore?

What will Sally pick up for you?

What did the children want?

What did Walter's car need?

What did the teacher ask for?

What did Mr. Jones take to work for lunch?

Extra Drill 2.8 **Nouns in a Series (Intonation)**

Repeat.

1. . . . a glass of milk

    . . . a sandwich and a glass of milk

    . . . he had a sandwich and a glass of milk

    For lunch he had a sandwich and a glass of milk.

2.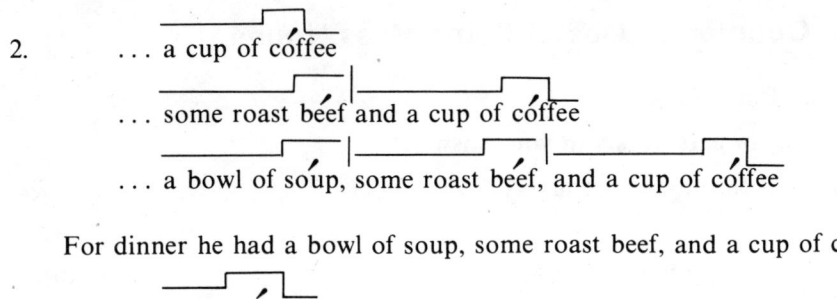

For dinner he had a bowl of soup, some roast beef, and a cup of coffee.

3.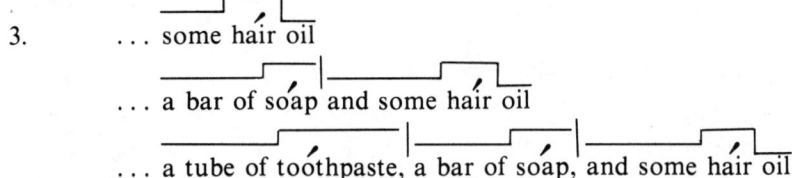

He bought a tube of toothpaste, a bar of soap, and some hair oil.

3 WORDS USED AS BOTH COUNT AND MASS NOUNS

Extra Drill 3.1 **Words Used as Both Count and Mass Nouns**

Complete the sentences with the words in parentheses.

1. There isn't .... here. Will someone please turn on .... for me?
   (a light, enough light)
2. .... has been very good this month for .... on River Street.
   (business, the businesses)
3. Mr. Burns didn't have .... in his office, so he had to rent .... for his secretary. *(another room, enough room)*
4. I always leave .... at .... on Maple Street.
   (my laundry, the laundry)
5. Here's an article in .... about the history of .... in Europe.
   (paper, the paper)

Extra Drill 3.2   **Countable Uses of Some Mass Nouns**

A. Foods as Mass and Count Nouns

Use one of the words in parentheses in your answer.

1. What did you eat for dinner last night? *(duck/ducks)*
   We ate duck.

2. What does Mr. Lane raise on his farm? *(duck/ducks)*
   He raises ducks.

3. What would you like for dessert today? *(pie/a pie)*
   ....

4. What did Johnny see in the garage? *(turkey/a turkey)*
   ....

5. What did the meat taste like? *(chicken/a chicken)*
   ....

6. What do you want with the ice cream? *(cake/cakes)*
   ....

B. Count Nouns Meaning "A kind of"

Answer the questions.

1. Is that paper expensive? *(heavy)*
   Yes, it's a heavy paper. Heavy papers are always expensive.

2. Is that coffee good? *(Colombian)*
   Yes, it's a Colombian coffee. Colombian coffees are always good.

3. Is that medicine expensive? *(new)*
   ....

4. Is that soup thin? *(American)*
   ....

5. Is that juice a little tart? *(unsweetened)*
   ....

6. Is that tobacco mild? *(Turkish)*
   ....

4 SOME NOUN MODIFIERS

Extra Drill 4.1 — **Adjectives as Noun Modifiers (Stress)**

A. Repeat. Notice the stress patterns.

réd shóes	hârd lésson	brôken ánkle
new clothes	black sweater	pretty garden
sharp knife	nice bracelet	easy lesson
long arms		

B. Complete the sentences.

1. Her shoes are red.
   She's wearing *red shoes*.

2. His clothes are new.
   He bought some *new clothes*.

3. This knife is sharp.
   This is a ....

4. His arms are long.
   What .... he has!

5. This lesson isn't hard.
   I don't think this is a ....

6. His sweater is black.
   Where did he get that ....

7. Her bracelet is nice.
   Her father gave her a ....

8. His ankle is broken.
   The doctor fixed his ....

9. That garden is pretty.
   What a .... that is!

10. This lesson is easy.
    What an .... this is!

Extra Drill 4.2 — **Premodifying Nouns (Stress)**

Change the phrases as in the examples. Use a premodifying noun.

	TEACHER	STUDENT
1.	a ring made of silver	a sîlver ríng
2.	some pants made of cotton	sóme côtton pánts
3.	some dresses made of wool	....
4.	a watch made of gold	....
5.	some spoons made of plastic	....
6.	a coat made of leather	....
7.	some money made of silver	....
8.	a door made of glass	....
9.	a bridge made of steel	....
10.	a tie pin made of gold	....

Extra Drill 4.3 **Premodifying Nouns**

JEWELER'S WINDOW

GOLD   SILVER

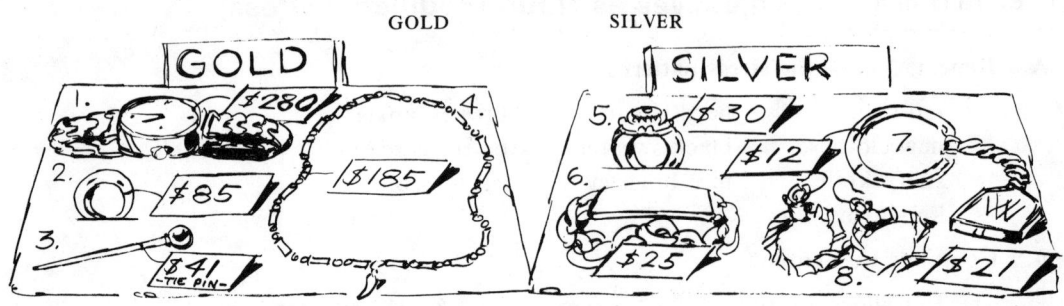

CLOTHING STORE WINDOW

"NEW FALL AND WINTER CLOTHING"—SALE

A. Answer the questions. Use a premodifying noun when possible.

   Examples:
   1. In the jeweler's window, what is the watch made of?
      It's made of gold.
   2. In the clothing store window, what sells for $39?
      The leather shoes (do).

B. When given a number, ask the price of the item using *how much*. Use a premodifying noun in each of your questions.

   Examples:

TEACHER	Item 1.
STUDENT A	*How much is the gold watch?*
STUDENT B	It is $280.
TEACHER	Item 13.
STUDENT A	*How much are the leather shoes?*
STUDENT B	They are $39.

| Extra Drill 4.4 | **Noun Possessives as Noun Modifiers**

Possessive endings (like noun plurals) are pronounced /-s/, /-z/, /-iz/. **Substitute.**

A. That's *Ruth's* /-s/ book.
    Beth's
    Kenneth's
    Luke's
    Phillip's
    Pat's

C. That's *Alice's* /-iz/ car.
    Joyce's
    Rose's
    George's
    Gus's
    Jess's

B. Isn't that *Ann's* /-z/ house?
    Carol's
    Bob's
    Tom's
    your friend's
    the professor's
    the Nelsons'

5 NOUN DETERMINERS

| Extra Drill 5.1 | **Noun Determiners (Introductory)**

Substitute progressively.

	You'll find *a map* in the drawer.
another	You'll find another map in the drawer.
your	....
maps	....
three	....
some	....
soap	....
that	....
bar of soap	....
one	....
another	....
box of napkins	You'll find another box of napkins in the drawer.

6 ARTICLES AND DEMONSTRATIVES; *some, any, no*

Extra Drill 6.1   Noun Determiners *a* (or *an*) and *the*

Complete each sentence with one indefinite article *(a/an)* and one definite article *(the)*.

1. Call .... police in .... emergency.
2. .... truck hit .... fence right here.
3. There might be .... fire down .... street.
4. Do you see .... penny on .... floor?
5. .... next street has .... very good Chinese restaurant.
6. Henrietta put .... bowl of flowers on .... dining room table.
7. .... ceiling has .... large brown spot on it.
8. Jimmy found .... package of gum in .... top drawer.
9. .... history teacher couldn't recommend .... book on labor unions.
10. We sent .... catalog yesterday, but you probably won't get it until .... day after tomorrow.

Extra Drill 6.2   Noun Determiners *some* and *any* with Plural

Answer the questions of Speaker A using a plural noun phrase. Use *some* as the plural of *a*.

SPEAKER A	SPEAKER B
1. Is the boy tired? (girls)	No, but the girls are tired.
2. Did they send a man? (woman)	No, but they sent some women.
3. Did Bob catch a turtle? (fish)	....
4. Did Tom lose the pen? (pencils)	....
5. Does Mary have a pad of paper? (notebooks)	....
6. Does Helen have an eggbeater? (sharp knives)	....
7. Did you see the package? (ribbons)	....
8. Did a package come this morning? (letters)	....
9. Is the meat burned? (potatoes)	....
10. Have you tried the salad? (pickles)	....

| Extra Drill 6.3 | **Noun Determiners** *some* **and** *any* **with Plural and Mass Nouns** |

Take the part of Speaker B. Use *some* **and** *any*.

1. SPEAKER A Did she buy any fruit?
   SPEAKER B Yes, she did.
   SPEAKER A Did she get oranges and grapes?
   SPEAKER B Well, she got *some oranges,* but she didn't get *any grapes.*

2. SPEAKER A Do the students have anything to write with?
   SPEAKER B Yes, they do.
   SPEAKER A Do they have pencils and pens?
   SPEAKER B Well, they have ...., but they don't have ....

3. SPEAKER A Did you stop at the filling station?
   SPEAKER B ....
   SPEAKER A Did you need gas and oil?
   SPEAKER B ....

4. SPEAKER A Did the furniture store have what you wanted?
   SPEAKER B ....
   SPEAKER A Did they have floor lamps and desk lamps?
   SPEAKER B ....

5. SPEAKER A Doesn't he have a lot of animals on his farm?
   SPEAKER B ....
   SPEAKER A Does he have cows and horses?
   SPEAKER B ....

6. SPEAKER A Did you get some things at the store?
   SPEAKER B ....
   SPEAKER A Did you get bread and milk?
   SPEAKER B ....

Extra Drill 6.4 — **Noun Determiners *some* and *any* in Questions**

Change the tag questions to negative questions using *some* or *any*. Complete the short answers.

	SPEAKER A	SPEAKER B
1.	You need some help, don't you?	
	Don't you need some help?	Yes, I do.
2.	Mother didn't bake any bread, did she?	
	Didn't Mother bake any bread?	No, she didn't.
3.	He doesn't want any carrots, does he?	
	....	No, ...
4.	She bought some new clothes, didn't she?	
	....	Yes, ...
5.	You have some homework, don't you?	
	....	Yes, ...
6.	You don't need any help, do you?	
	....	No, ...
7.	There weren't any policemen there, were there?	
	....	No, ...
8.	We don't have any homework, do we?	
	....	No, ...
9.	You need some money, don't you?	
	....	Yes, ...
10.	He doesn't have any friends, does he?	
	....	No, ...

| Extra Drill 6.5 | **Noun Determiners** *no* **and** *not...any* |

A. Repeat the sentence and then, using the cue, form a second sentence using *not...any*.

1. Johnny would eat no string beans. (carrots)
   He wouldn't eat any carrots either.

2. I have no scissors. (thread)
   I don't have any thread either.

3. They had no cows on their farm. (horses)
   ....

4. They had no fresh eggs. (fresh bread)
   ....

5. There are no good magazines for sale. (books)
   ....

6. I've received no letters from him. (telephone calls)
   ....

7. He brought no flowers for her. (candy)
   ....

8. There were no photographers there. (reporters)
   ....

B. Now use the determiner *no* before the noun phrase in your second sentence.

1. They don't have any children. (pets)
   They have no pets either.

2. The store didn't have any light bulbs. (batteries)
   It had no batteries either.

3. There weren't any good hotels there. (motels)
   ....

4. I haven't read any good biographies lately. (novels)
   ....

5. There weren't any pictures on the classroom wall. (maps)
   ....

6. He doesn't eat any kind of meat. (seafood)
   ....

7. The car didn't have any tires. (motor)
   ....

8. There wasn't any rice. (tea)
   ....

8 NOUN MODIFIERS: PREPOSITIONAL PHRASES

Extra Drill 8.1 — Prepositional Phrases as Noun Modifiers

Substitute.

That tall building *in the next block* is the new post office.
                  on the corner
                  on Fifth Street
                  near the river
                  across the street
                  in front of us

Extra Drill 8.2 — Prepositional Phrases as Noun Modifiers

Combine the sentences into one sentence.

1. You can use the desk.
   The desk is in the living room.
         You can use the desk in the living room.

2. The sandwiches are in this sack.
   The sandwiches are yours.
         The sandwiches in this sack are yours.

3. Why don't you go to the bank?
   The bank is on the corner.
   ....

4. Let's go to the cafeteria.
   The cafeteria is in the next block.
   ....

5. The chalk is in this box.
   The chalk is yellow.
   ....

6. Will you mail the letters?
   The letters are on the table.
   ....

7. The cream is in that bottle
   The cream is sour.
   ....

8. You can borrow the raincoat.
   The raincoat's in the closet.
   ....

| Extra Drill 8.3 | **Prepositional Phrases as Noun Modifiers** |

Form a noun phrase (NP) from (a). Combine (a) and (b) to form a sentence (S).

TEACHER STUDENT

1. (a) The girl has red hair. NP the girl with red hair.
   (b) She's John's sister. S The girl with red hair is John sister.

2. (a) The man isn't wearing a coat. NP the man without a coat
   (b) He's a farmer. S The man without a coat is a farmer.

3. (a) That woman has long fingernails. NP .....
   (b) She's an actress. S .....

4. (a) The man has long hair. NP .....
   (b) He's an artist. S .....

5. (a) The young woman's wearing a white uniform. NP .....
   (b) She's a nurse. S .....

6. (a) The young man isn't wearing a tie. NP .....
   (b) He couldn't enter the restaurant. S .....

7. (a) The tall man's wearing glasses. NP .....
   (b) He's a professor. S .....

8. (a) The young woman is carrying a red purse. NP .....
   (b) She's a French teacher. S .....

9. (a) The lady's wearing black stockings. NP .....
   (b) She isn't very young. S .....

10. (a) The man's wearing a white helmet. NP .....
    (b) He's a policeman. S .....

9 PRONOUNS

| Extra Drill 9.1 | **Subject and Object Pronouns** |

Complete the sentences.

1. I saw him, and *he saw me.*
2. He looked at her, and *she looked at him.*
3. I promised her, and .....
4. We asked them, and .....
5. He chose her, and .....

6. I embarrassed you, and ....
7. They need us, and ....
8. He loves her, and ....
9. He hated me, and ....
10. They watched us, and ....
11. I listened to her, and ....
12. He understood them, and ....
13. She believed us, and ....
14. We visited them, and ....
15. He remembered her, and ....

| Extra Drill 9.2 | **Subject and Object Pronouns** |

Answer the questions. Use the cued verb and use pronouns.

SPEAKER A	SPEAKER B
1. What about the young woman with red hair and the old man with glasses? *(spoke)*	She spoke to him.
2. What about the short boy with long hair and the tall girl with short hair? *(loves)*	....
3. What about Mary's little brother and his cat? *(was looking for)*	....
4. What about that little boy and his glasses? *(is always breaking)*	....
5. What about Sally and those chocolate cookies? *(made)*	....
6. What about wool clothing and Mrs. Faye? *(itches)*	....
7. What about success and Rock Hunter? *(spoiled)*	....
8. What about all the neighborhood children and your new green rug? *(walked all over)*	....
9. What about you and that new secretary in Mr. Kimura's office? *(ride the bus with)*	....
10. What about Abraham Lincoln and the slaves? *(freed)*	....

10 NOUN DETERMINERS; *more* and *most; enough; plenty of*

Extra Drill 10.1 **Noun Determiner *enough***

Substitute.

A. They don't have enough móney.
      food
      clothing
      room
      railroads
      universities
      hospitals

B. She made cóffee enough for éveryone.
      tea
      soup
      cookies
      stew
      sandwiches
      coffee and sandwiches

Extra Drill 10.2 **Noun Determiner *enough***

Change the position of *enough*.

1. They don't have enough fóod.
   They don't have fóod enough.

2. We don't have cóffee enough.
   We don't have enough cóffee.

3. We didn't receive informátion enough.
   ....

4. We've had enough tróuble.
   ....

5. She didn't make bréad enough.
   ....

6. The teacher gave us enough hómework.
   ....

7. We have róom enough.
   ....

8. Farmers never have enough hélp.
   ....

9. They said they didn't have enough men to finish the jób.
   ....

10. The newspaper doesn't have enough repórters.
    ....

11 NOUN DETERMINERS: *a lot of* and *lots of; much/many; a little/a few; a great (good) deal of*

Extra Drill 11.1	**Noun Determiners: *a lot of* and *lots of***

A. Answer the questions according to the statements of fact.

> **STATEMENT OF FACT**
> 1. There are a lot of record stores.
> 2. There were a lot of musicians at the hotel.
> 3. We saw a lot of good books on sale.
> 4. We found a lot of dead birds.
> 5. They served a lot of tea and coffee.
> 6. I use a lot of face powder.

	SPEAKER A	SPEAKER B
1.	Are there a lot of music stores?	No, but there are a lot of record stores.
2.	Were there a lot of artists at the hotel?	....
3.	Did you see a lot of records on sale?	....
4.	Did you find a lot of dead fish?	....
5.	Did they serve a lot of beer?	....
6.	Do you use a lot of rouge?	....

B. Answer the questions. Put loud stress on *lots* for emphasis.

	SPEAKER A	SPEAKER B
1.	Have you had much rain recently?	Yes, we've had lóts of rain recently.
2.	Have they hired more policemen recently?	....
3.	Have they recently lost any equipment?	....
4.	Have you gotten any new friends recently?	....
5.	Have you sold much yellow paint recently?	....
6.	Have they investigated many of those reports recently?	....

| **Extra Drill 11.2** | **Noun Determiners:** *many* **and** *much* |

Change these sentences to the negative, using *much* **or** *many* **in the transformed sentence.**

1. There were a lot of people there.
   There weren't many people there.

2. He has lots of homework tonight.
   He doesn't have much homework tonight.

3. There were a lot of photographers there.
   ....

4. We had a lot of trouble.
   ....

5. That building has lots of windows.
   ....

6. He has a lot of shoes.
   ....

7. I take lots of medicine.
   ....

8. I receive a lot of letters.
   ....

9. They have lots of money.
   ....

10. There are a lot of boats on the river today.
    ....

11. I have a lot of time.
    ....

12. That boy has lots of toys.
    ....

| **Extra Drill 11.3** | **Noun Determiners:** *little* **and** *few* |

Say the sentences again, using *little* **or** *few*.

1. He doesn't have very many friends.
   He has few friends.

2. They don't have very much money.
   They have little money.

3. She doesn't have very much interest in science.
   ....

4. There weren't many hospitals there.
   ....

5. The hotel didn't have very many guests.
   ....

6. I haven't had much experience.
   ....

7. There aren't very many good dictionaries.
   ....

8. There weren't many good athletes there.
   ....

9. The building was burning, but there wasn't much smoke.
   ....

10. He didn't have very much education.
    ....

12 NOUN SUBSTITUTES

Extra Drill 12.1 **Noun Substitutes** *many, much, a little, a few*

Take the part of Speaker B and answer the questions.

	SPEAKER A	SPEAKER B
1.	How many people came?	Not many. Just a few.
2.	How much sugar do you use in your tea?	Not much. Just a little.
3.	How many oranges should I get when I go to the store?	....
4.	How much homework do you have tonight?	....
5.	How many boys were there in the park?	....
6.	How much English does she know?	....
7.	How much work do you have?	....
8.	How many songs can you sing?	....
9.	How much money do you need?	....
10.	How many gifts did she get?	....

| Extra Drill 12.2 | **Noun Substitutes (Quantity, Demonstratives)**

Say the sentences again, using a noun substitute for the italicized words.

1. He lost *a great deal of money.*
   He lost a great deal.
2. There's *no butter.*
   There is none.
3. Why don't you try *this pen?*
   Why don't you try this (one)?
4. He eats *a lot of food.*
   ....
5. Why won't you sell me *those apples.*
   ....
6. He offered me *some candy.*
   ....
7. I've had *enough coffee,* thank you.
   ....
8. He ate *two pieces of candy.*
   ....
9. *Five people* came.
   ....
10. I think *this car* is the best.
    ....
11. He doesn't do *a great deal of work.*
    ....
12. *Many people* were swimming.
    ....
13. *Several hotels* were almost empty.
    ....
14. He told us *a lot of information.*
    ....
15. He makes *a great deal of money.*
    ....

| Extra Drill 12.3 | **Noun Substitutes (Possessive Pronouns)** |

Take the part of Speaker B and answer the questions.

SPEAKER A   SPEAKER B

A. 1. Is this Jim's book?   I think it's his.

   2. Are these our books?   I think they're ours.

   3. Is this Mary's money?   I think it's hers.

   4. Is this your pen?   ....

   5. Is this my book?   ....

   6. Are those Helen's glasses?   ....

   7. Are these our raincoats?   ....

   8. Is that their house?   ....

   9. Are these your shoes?   ....

B. 1. Is that your pen?   It looks like mine.

   2. Are these Bob's glasses?   They look like his.

   3. Is that Mary's hat?   ....

   4. Is this your umbrella?   ....

   5. Is that Tom's bike?   ....

   6. Are those our children?   ....

   7. Is that your watch?   ....

   8. Are those his tickets?   ....

   9. Is this their camera?   ....

14 ADJECTIVE PRECEDENCE

| Extra Drill 14.1 | **Adjective Precedence (Stress)** |

Listen and repeat.

1. a comfortable blue sofa
   a serious young boy
   an important new discovery
   some clean white sheets
   a crowded little street

2. a pretty little blue ring
   some interesting old red stamps
   a dirty old black truck
   a nice new green dress

| **Extra Drill 14.2** | **Adjective Precedence** |

Add the adjective modifiers progressively.

	TEACHER	STUDENT
1.	He lives in a house.	
	white	He lives in a white house.
	beautiful	He lives in a beautiful white house.
	old	He lives in a beautiful old white house.
2.	She's wearing a hat.	
	funny	....
	pink	....
	little	....
3.	I saw a fire engine.	
	red	....
	beautiful	....
	new	....
4.	She's wearing a pin.	
	interesting	....
	little	....
	red	....
5.	I caught a fish.	
	little	....
	blue	....
	strange	....
6.	I took a picture of a church.	
	old	....
	interesting	....
	white	....
7.	He bought a boat.	
	white	....
	new	....
	wonderful	....

| Extra Drill 14.3 | **Adjective Precedence** |

Progressive addition of modifiers.

1. She bought an old painting.
   - old — She bought an old painting.
   - beautiful — She bought a beautiful old painting.
   - French — She bought a beautiful old French painting.

2. He drives a car.
   - Italian ....
   - little ....
   - fast ....

3. He has a camera.
   - expensive ....
   - new ....
   - Japanese ....

4. He's an architect.
   - famous ....
   - Brazilian ....
   - young ....

5. We saw a film.
   - interesting ....
   - very ....
   - Canadian ....

15 NOUN DETERMINERS *some* AND *any* WITH STRONG STRESS

| Extra Drill 15.1 | **Noun Determiners *some* and *any* with Strong Stress** |

Read the responses filling *some* or *any* in the blanks.

1. What company makes these toys?
   I think they're made by *sóme* cómpany in St. Louis.

2. Who cooked this dish? It's delicious!
   I think it was cooked by *sóme* stúdent from Vietnam.

3. Where's Mr. Clark from?
   He comes from .... state in the West. I don't remember which one.

4. Was everyone surprised?
   Oh, yes. There isn't .... normal person who wouldn't be surprised.

5. Please deliver it tomorrow, Mr. Conrad.
   There must be .... mistake. My name isn't Conrad.

6. How was she killed?
   They don't know, but .... weapon with a sharp point was used.

7. Have you got everything you need?
   Almost. I still have to buy .... green vegetables.

8. What can we do about it?
   I don't know. There doesn't seem to be .... way to get out of it.

9. Your equipment is terribly expensive.
   I know. We're looking for .... way to make it less expensive.

10. My bank account doesn't balance.
    Then you've made .... mistake. Add it up again.

11. Do you believe them?
    I don't have .... reason to doubt what they told me.

12. Are we lost, Fred?
    Oh, no. I think they live in .... house around here, dear.

16 NOUN DETERMINERS: *either/neither; another/other; each* and *every*

| Extra Drill 16.1 | **Noun Determiners *either* and *neither*** |

Respond to Speaker A's statement using *not...either*.

	SPEAKER A	SPEAKER B
1.	He took neither book.	You mean he didn't take either one?
2.	I told neither boy.	You mean you didn't tell either one?
3.	I heard neither child.	....
4.	I saw neither movie.	....
5.	We heard neither speech.	....
6.	He'll finish neither experiment.	....
7.	I can find neither child.	....
8.	She could understand neither speaker.	....

| Extra Drill 16.2 | **Noun Substitutes** *another* **and** *others* |

Use *another* **or** *others* **as noun substitutes.**

TEACHER	STUDENT
1. Another boy arrived.	Another arrived.
2. Other people are coming.	Others are coming.
3. Were there other people there?	........................?
4. Please have another orange.	....
5. Are there other elevators?	........................?
6. Is there another restaurant?	........................?
7. Other experiments failed.	....
8. Are there other ideas?	........................?
9. Do you have another alarm clock?	........................?
10. I'd like another piece of candy.	....

| Extra Drill 16.3 | **Noun Substitutes** *the other* **and** *the others* |

Use *the other* **or** *the others* **as noun substitutes.**

TEACHER	STUDENT
1. The other tape's over there.	The other's over there.
2. The other glasses are dirty.	The others are dirty.
3. The other classroom is empty.	....
4. What were the other conditions?	....
5. The other guests are arriving.	....
6. Have you seen the other children?	....
7. The other dress is prettier.	....
8. The other picture's better.	....
9. The other pictures are better.	....
10. The other medicine's on the table.	....

| Extra Drill 16.4 | **Noun Determiners** *every* **and** *each* |

Change the sentences using the determiner *each*.

1. I gave a book to every student in the class.
   Each student received a book.
2. I gave an apple to every child in the room.
   Each child received an apple.
3. She gave a gift to every child at the party.
   ....
4. She wrote a letter to every child in the hospital.
   ....
5. He gave a flower to every lady at the party.
   ....
6. The hotel gave one free meal to every guest.
   ....
7. Mr. Jones gave every employee one hundred dollars.
   ....
8. Mary sent an invitation to every child in her class.
   ....

| Extra Drill 16.5 | **Noun Determiners Before** *one* **(Stress)** |

A. After *another, the other, this* and *that*, the word *one* has weak stress.

B. After *either, neither, each* and *every*, the word *one* often has strong stress.

1. **Listen.** 　　this one 　　that one 　　another one 　　the other one	1. **Listen.** 　　each one 　　either one 　　neither one 　　every one
2. **Repeat.** 　　I'd like this one. 　　Give me that one. 　　Take another one. 　　Try the other one.	2. **Repeat.** 　　Try each one. 　　Take either one. 　　I wanted neither one. 　　He tried every one.

17 INDEFINITE PRONOUNS

> **Extra Drill 17.1**   **Indefinite Pronouns (Stress)**

All indefinite pronouns are stressed on the first syllable. *-one* and *-thing* usually have weak stress. Listen and repeat.

ányone	ánything	ánybody
éveryone	éverything	éverybody
sómeone	sómething	sómebody
nó one	nóthing	nóbody

1. Don't tell anyone.
2. We told no one.
3. I don't know anything.
4. He said nothing.
5. I don't see anybody.
6. She told everybody.

> **Extra Drill 17.2**   **Indefinite Pronouns *some-, any-, no-***

A. Repeat the cued sentence and form a negative second sentence using the cued subject.

	TEACHER	STUDENT
1.	I saw somebody. (He)	I saw somebody. He didn't see anybody.
2.	She heard something. (I)	She heard something. I didn't hear anything.
3.	He'll tell someone. (I)	....
4.	She lost something. (We)	....
5.	He's decided something. (She)	....
6.	They've invited someone. (We)	....

B. Repeat the cued sentence and form a second sentence. Use the cued subject and the pronouns *no one, nobody* or *nothing*.

	TEACHER	STUDENT
1.	He didn't see anyone. (I)	He didn't see anyone. I saw no one either.
2.	She won't tell anybody. (Joe)	I won't tell anybody. Joe will tell nobody either.
3.	I won't borrow anything. (Ann)	....
4.	Karl doesn't believe anyone. (We)	....
5.	They didn't buy anything. (I)	....
6.	Susan couldn't hear anything. (Carol)	....

| Extra Drill 17.3 | **Possessive Indefinite Pronouns** |

A. Answer the question with the cued words. Follow the models.

What did you find?

	TEACHER	STUDENT
1.	umbrella	Somebody's umbrella.
2.	raincoat	Somebody's raincoat.
3.	bracelet	....
4.	tennis racket	....
5.	passport	....
6.	suit coat	....
7.	wallet	....
8.	camera	....
9.	ice skates	....

B. Complete the answers with *somebody's, anybody's, everybody's* or *nobody's*.

1.	Did the thieves take all the jewels?	Yes, they took *everybody's*.
2.	Does anyone own the little white dog?	No, it's ....
3.	Who owns the big brown and white dog?	I don't know, but it must be ....
4.	And how about this little long-haired cat?	That doesn't seem to be .... either.
5.	Did they get the same gift?	Yes, I think .... is the same.

| Extra Drill 17.4 | **Possessive Indefinite *somebody else's*** |

Answer the questions. Note the stress emphasis.

	SPEAKER A	SPEAKER B
1.	Is this her passport?	No, that passport isn't hers. It's somebody else's.
2.	Are these your pencils?	No, those pencils aren't mine. They're somebody's else's.
3.	Is this my package?	No, ...
4.	Is this his ring?	No, ...

5. Is this their camera?   No, ...
....

6. Is this our ball?   No, ...
....

7. Is this your raincoat?   No, ...
....

8. Are these her shoes?   No, ...
....

| Extra Drill 17.5 | **Indefinite Pronouns Modified by Adjectives** |

A. **Substitute progressively.**

	For this job we need someone capable.
experienced	....
musical	....
intelligent	....
very tall	....
different	....
something	....
heavier	....
Let's put on	....
warm	....
comfortable	....
nice	Let's put on something nice.

B. **Substitute progressively.**

	We never do anything interesting.
exciting	....
dangerous	....
different	....
Do you know	....
new	....
funny	....
anyone	....
artistic	....
rich	....
famous	....
unusual	Do you know anyone unusual?

| Extra Drill 17.6 | **Indefinite Pronouns Modified by Prepositional Phrases**

Repeat.

A.
1. Someone on the telephone wants to speak with you.
2. Someone at the door wants to sell us something.
3. Someone from the newspaper is asking about the accident.
4. Someone on the bus is waving at you.
5. Someone across the street is calling to you.

B.
1. Everyone in the street was running.
2. Everyone on the bus was angry.
3. Everyone in the field of education was at the meeting.
4. Everyone in the picture was smiling.
5. Everyone at the party was having a good time.

19 NOUN DETERMINERS: *all (the)* and *both (the)*

| Extra Drill 19.1 | **Noun Determiner** *all (the)*

Change the sentences. Follow the models.

1. All the men work hard.
   The men all work hard.

2. All the children were very good.
   The children were all very good.

3. All the women were talking.
   ....

4. All the men on the bus were reading newspapers.
   ....

5. All the cars in the street stopped.
   ....

6. All the windows in the house were broken.
   ....

7. All the jewelry was expensive.
   ....

8. All languages are difficult.
   ....

9. All the packages arrived.
   ....

10. All sugar is sweet.
    ....

11. All lemons are sour.
    ....

12. All the knives are sharp.
    ....

| Extra Drill 19.2 | *They all* **and** *they both* |

Use a pronoun subject + *all* or *both* in the reply.

SPEAKER A	SPEAKER B
1. Did the two boys go?	Yes, they both went.
2. Did all the men say that?	Yes, they all said that.
3. Have the three girls gone to bed?	Yes, they've all gone to bed.
4. Were the two hikers lost?	Yes, ...
5. Do your two sisters know how to cook?	Yes, ...
6. Are all three of your brothers married?	Yes, ...
7. Did all the children come?	Yes, ...
8. Did all the typewriter ribbons arrive?	Yes, ...
9. Did both men take the bus?	Yes, ...
10. Do all the professors at the university teach classes?	Yes, ...
11. Are all the hotels full?	Yes, ...

20 PREDETERMINERS

Extra Drill 20.1 **Predeterminer** *each*

Change the sentences.

A.
1. Each of the boys has a bicycle.
   The boys each have a bicycle.

2. Each of the men gave a report.
   The men each gave a report.

3. Each of the ladies was wearing a white dress.
   ....

4. Each of the children brought a gift.
   ....

5. Each of the rooms was filled with flowers.
   ....

6. Each of the photographers took several pictures.
   ....

B.
1. Each of the men gave a report.
   Each man gave a report.

2. Each of the wives stayed with her husband.
   Each wife stayed with her husband.

3. Each of the children chose a toy.
   ....

4. Each of the policemen works eight hours.
   ....

5. Each of the women bought a ticket.
   ....

6. Each of the loaves of bread was baked today.
   ....

| Extra Drill 20.2 | **Predeterminer** *every one* |

Change the sentences. Use *every one* as a determiner. Use a past participle (broken, filled, etc.).

TEACHER	STUDENT
1. Joey broke all his toys.	Every one of his toys is broken now.
2. I filled all the gas tanks.	Every one of the gas tanks is filled now.
3. The rain spoiled all the strawberries.	....
4. Kim washed all the dishes.	....
5. Mr. Adams closed all the windows.	....
6. Mrs. Adams locked all the doors.	....
7. The police changed all the locks.	....
8. Sam finished all his tests.	....
9. I emptied all my pockets.	....
10. Fred painted all the chairs.	....

| Extra Drill 20.3 | **Predeterminers** |

Complete these sentences with *one* (if necessary) + *of* and a pronoun.

1. I didn't like the food. I didn't eat much *of it*.
2. Do you know his two sisters? Do you know either *(one) of them?*
3. I worked all the problems. I think I've correctly solved every ....
4. The oranges looked good so I bought a few ....
5. He doesn't spend all his money. He tries to save a little ....
6. I like to read the newspaper. I always read all ....
7. I didn't like the meat. I couldn't eat any ....
8. I like the apples so I ate every ....
9. George likes country music. He listens to a great deal ....
10. The last exams were easy. I passed every ....
11. The two girls are nice. I like both ....
12. I didn't like the wine so I didn't drink much ....
13. The pens were very cheap so I bought several ....

21 ADJECTIVE + *one* or *ones*

Extra Drill 21.1   **Adjective + *one(s)* (Stress)**

After an adjective, *one* and *ones* have weak stress. Listen and repeat.

A.
- a blúe òne
- a shórt òne
- a láte òne
- sòme gréen ònes
- some óld ònes
- some ólder ònes

B.
- a blúe swèater and a bláck òne
- a lóng book and a shórt òne
- an éarly tràin and a láte òne
- sòme góod idèas and sòme bád ònes
- some néw shòes and some óld ònes
- some yóung chìldren and some ólder ònes

22 PRE-NOUN MODIFIERS (SUMMARY)

Extra Drill 22.1   **Order of Pre-Noun Modifiers**

Add all the modifiers. Add them in the correct order.

Example: He's an .... engineer. *(Colombian, intelligent, young)*
             He's an intelligent, young, Colombian engineer.

1. We discovered a .... restaurant. *(charming, French, old)*
2. The garden was full of .... statues. *(marble, uninteresting, white)*
3. She was .... architect. *(Brazilian, a, talented)*
4. The professor identified it as an .... lion. *(ancient, Cambodian, stone)*
5. I was able to buy a .... bell. *(brass, oriental, valuable)*
6. There's nothing like a .... orange. *(big, Florida, juicy)*
7. .... cars were in the accident. *(foreign, several, small)*

24 SENTENCES AS OBJECTS OF TRANSITIVE VERBS

Extra Drill 24.1   **Sentence as Object of *say***

Answer in the negative, stressing the auxiliary and using object pronouns. Omit the subordinator *that*.

1. Did he say that he could come?   No. He said he cóuldn't come.
2. Did she say that she knew John?   No. She said she dídn't know him.
3. Did they say that they saw the movie?   ....
4. Did she say that she could help us?   ....
5. Did he say that he wrote the letter?   ....

6. Did they say that they invited Barbara? ....
7. Did he say that the noise bothered him? ....
8. Did she say that she went to the dance? ....

25 DIRECT SPEECH

Extra Drill 25.1 **Direct Speech Quotations**

Listen carefully to these readings of direct speech that have reporting tags. Notice the intonation patterns. Repeat each sentence.

1. Her mother said, "Come in the kitchen."
2. "Come in the kitchen," her mother said.
3. "Come in the kitchen," her mother said, "and finish your soup."
4. "I'm going back to the car," said Sal.
5. "I'm going back to the car," said Sal, "because I left my keys there."
6. Casper asked timidly, "Are men allowed here?"
7. "Are men allowed here?" Casper asked timidly.
8. "Are men allowed here," Casper asked timidly, "if there's no room over there?"
9. "Will you raise your right hand?" asked the judge finally.
10. "Will you raise your right hand," asked the judge, "and repeat after me?"

26 INDIRECT SPEECH

Extra Drill 26.1 **Indirect Speech**

Take the part of the Reporter. Use the subordinator *that*.

SPEAKER	REPORTER
1. The car is getting old. What does Jerry always say?	He always says that the car is getting old.
2. The window is stuck. What does Amelia always say?	....
3. Tom is never on time. What does Aunt Polly always say?	....
4. Christmas is a humbug. What does Uncle Scrooge always say?	....

5. The water's too cold.
   What does Miss Kelly always say? ....

6. Meat is too expensive.
   What does Mrs. Cunningham always say? ....

7. People should get more exercise.
   What does Mr. Hamilton always say? ....

8. The maid will do it tomorrow.
   What does Mrs. Hamilton always say? ....

9. A smart dog can learn anything.
   What does Mr. Casey always say? ....

10. You can't teach an old dog new tricks.
    What does his son always say? ....

27 INDIRECT SPEECH: VERB FORMS AND TENSES

Extra Drill 27.1   **Past Tense in Indirect Speech**

Complete the sentences. Use past tense.

1. Tom: "I'm late."
   He said *he was late*.

2. Mary: "I want to go."
   She told me *she wanted to go*.

3. Dr. Jones: "I'm going to the hospital."
   He told his secretary ....

4. Mrs. Smith: "I don't need anything at the store."
   She said ....

5. Bob: "I think it's going to rain."
   He said ....

6. Mr. Wilson: "I believe it's time for me to go."
   He said ....

7. Professor White: "I'm sure Fred knows the answer."
   He told the class ....

8. Lisa: "I'm glad to hear that."
   She said ....

9. Mrs. Flower: "I think Doris is going to marry Henry."
   She told Mrs. Jones ....

10. Alan: "I think Lydia is in my science class."
    He said ....

11. June: "I'm not sure when I'm going to leave."
    She told me ....

12. Steve: "I don't think it's my mistake."
    He told us ....

| Extra Drill 27.2 | **Past Modals in Indirect Speech** |

Take the part of the Reporter. Report the statements, using pronouns as appropriate.

Examples:

1. MARY   "I can't see the blackboard."

   What did Mary say?

   REPORTER   She said she couldn't see the blackboard.

2. BARBARA   "I'll call you soon, Helen."

   What did Barbara tell Helen?

   REPORTER   She told her she'd call her soon.

Continue.

| Extra Drill 27.3 | **Past Modals in Indirect Speech** |

A. Report what John said to Mary.

                                              REPORTER
1. "I must study."   He told her he had to study.
2. "I can't go."   He told her he couldn't go.
3. "I'd like to go to the Far East."   ....
4. "I'll fix the tape for you."   ....
5. "You should have more patience."   ....
6. "You may use my book."   ....

B. Report what John said to you (the reporter).

                                              REPORTER
1. 'I'll give you a ring."   He told me he'd give me a ring.
2. "I can't take the exam."   ....
3. 'I'd like to go to the Far East."   ....
4. "You have to practice all the time."   ....
5. "You must be on time."   ....
6. "You'll like the new English teacher."   ....

Extra Drill 27.4 **Past Perfect in Indirect Speech**

Use the past perfect (*had* + past participle) when reporting what is said.

1. Tom: "I haven't seen her."
   He said *he hadn't seen her.*

2. Bill: "I've never studied Spanish."
   He said ....

3. Mary: "I haven't finished yet, Helen."
   She told Helen ....

4. Mrs. White: "I've never met Doris, Mrs. Jones."
   She told Mrs. Jones ....

5. Dr. Farmer: "Three students haven't taken the exam yet."
   He said ....

6. Mrs. White: "I haven't done the dishes yet."
   She said ....

7. Tom: "I haven't told anyone, Bob."
   He told Bob ....

8. Mrs. Jones: "All the food has spoiled."
   She said ....

9. Mrs. Green: "Tom's gone to school, Bill."
   She told Bill ....

10. Henry: "I haven't eaten lunch, George."
    He told George ....

28 INDIRECT SPEECH: CHOICE OF TENSES

Extra Drill 28.1 **Present Tense after *said* in Indirect Speech**

In reporting these statements, use the present tense in the subordinate clause to show that the statements are still true at the time of reporting.

1. CARLOS   "I always speak Spanish with my friends."
   TEACHER   Did you understand what Carlos said?
   REPORTER   Yes, he said he always speaks Spanish with his friends.
2. MR. ODA   "I live in one of the most beautiful countries in the world."
   TEACHER   Excuse me. I didn't hear what Mr. Oda said. Did you?
   REPORTER   Yes, he said ....

Continue.

| Extra Drill 28.2 | **Present Perfect after *said* in Indirect Speech** |

When reporting these statements, use the present perfect (*have/has* + past participle) in the subordinate clause to show that the action continues at the time of reporting.

MR. SAN   "I've lived here for two years."

TEACHER   Excuse me. What did Mr. San say?

LISTENER   He said he's lived here for two years.
(REPORTER)

Continue.

29 Wh- QUESTION WORDS

Extra Drill 29.1 **Question Words** *which* **and** *whose* **+ NP**

Respond to Speaker A with a question beginning with *which* or *whose* + NP.

	SPEAKER A	SPEAKER B
1.	This isn't my pen.	Whose pen is it?
2.	He doesn't live in that house.	Which house does he live in?
3.	That's not Mr. Farmer's car.	.... ?
4.	Those aren't Mary's ice skates.	.... ?
5.	I don't want that book.	.... ?
6.	I didn't come in that car.	.... ?
7.	That's not my package.	.... ?
8.	I didn't come in Tom's car.	.... ?
9.	He's not staying at that hotel.	.... ?
10.	Your shirts aren't in the top drawer.	.... ?
11.	Those handkerchiefs aren't yours.	.... ?

| Extra Drill 29.2 | **Question Words** *who, what, when, where, why, how* |

Speaker A: Form a question-word based on the statement of fact. Use the italicized NP or adverbial as a guide to which question word to use.

Speaker B: Reply with a short answer based on the statement of fact.

> **STATEMENT OF FACT**
> 1. He went *downtown*.
> 2. *Bob* answered the question.
> 3. That's *a tape recorder*.
> 4. Tom's writing *a letter*.
> 5. He left *because he was tired*.
> 6. The bus leaves *at eight o'clock*.
> 7. I saw *Jane* at the movies.
> 8. He always travels *by plane*.
> 9. *Her sister* couldn't come.
> 10. She met *Ted's brother*.
> 11. He gave her *a bracelet*.
> 12. He's sleepy *because he stayed up late*.
> 13. They'll be back *tomorrow*.
> 14. He took *the package* to the post office.
> 15. They learn *by memorizing*.

SPEAKER A

1. Where did he go?
2. Who answered the question?
3. What's that?
4. ....?
5. ....?
6. ....?
7. ....?
8. ....?
9. ....?
10. ....?
11. ....?
12. ....?

SPEAKER B

Downtown.
Bob did.
A tape recorder.
....
....
....
....
....
....
....
....
....

13. ....? ....
14. ....? ....
15. ....? ....

| Extra Drill 29.3 | **Question Word *how* + Adjective** |

Speaker B: Form question-word questions using the cue. Base your questions on the italicized phrases in Speaker A's sentences.

1. SPEAKER A   It's *five miles* from the hotel to the airport. (bus station)
   SPEAKER B   How far is it from the hotel to the bus station?

2. SPEAKER A   He paid *two dollars* for that pen. (cigarette lighter)
   SPEAKER B   How much did he pay for the cigarette lighter?

3. SPEAKER A   The family room is *twenty-two feet long*. (living room)
   SPEAKER B   ....?

4. SPEAKER A   Bourbon Street is *twenty feet wide*. (Canal Street)
   SPEAKER B   ....?

5. SPEAKER A   This building is *six hundred feet high*. (that building)
   SPEAKER B   ....?

6. SPEAKER A   John is *six feet tall*. (Bob)
   SPEAKER B   ....?

7. SPEAKER A   She lived in Montreal *for a long time*. (there)
   SPEAKER B   ....?

8. SPEAKER A   It's *five miles* to Los Angeles. (San Francisco)
   SPEAKER B   ....?

9. SPEAKER A   John plays basketball *two times a week*. (play tennis)
   SPEAKER B   ....?

10. SPEAKER A   Bill weighs *one hundred pounds*. (his brother)
    SPEAKER B   ....?

30 INDIRECT QUESTIONS: *Wh-* QUESTIONS

| Extra Drill 30.1 | **Indirect *Wh-* Questions** |

Report the questions that Mr. Brown asked you (the reporter) during an interview.

MR. BROWN	REPORTER
1. How are you?	He asked me how I was.
2. What's your name?	He asked me what my name was.
3. What's your father's name?	....
4. What's your mother's name?	....
5. When were you born?	....
6. How old are you?	....
7. Where were you born?	....
8. Where do you live?	....
9. Where did you go to school?	....
10. What foreign languages do you speak?	....
11. How long have you studied English?	....

| Extra Drill 30.2 | **Indirect *Wh-* Questions** |

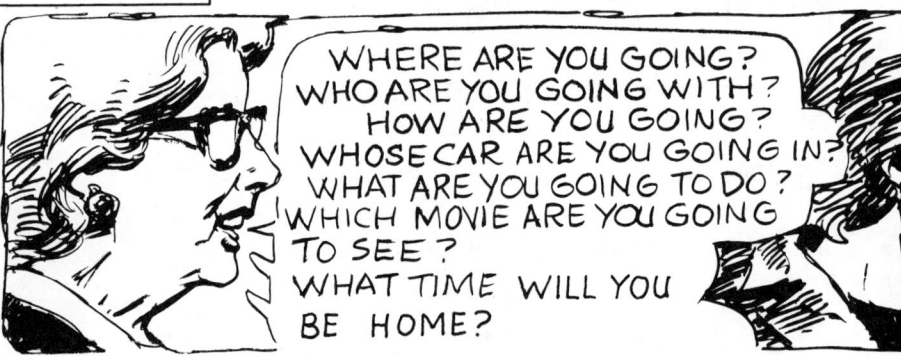

Report the questions that Mrs. Farmer asked her son.

1. MRS. FARMER "Where are you going?"
   REPORTER She asked him where he was going.
2. MRS. FARMER "Who are you going with?"
   REPORTER She asked him who he was going with.

Continue.

Extra Drill 30.3   **Indirect Wh- Questions**

Report the questions that these people asked.

1. Mrs. Brown asked Tom where his mother was.
2. ....
3. ....
4. ....
5. ....
6. ....
7. ....
8. ....
9. ....
10. ....

| Extra Drill 30.4 | **Indirect Wh- Questions** |

1. TOM: "Where's your bike, Bill?"
2. MARY: "When did you sell your car, Ted?"
3. ALICE: "Where did Helen go, Mary?"
4. HENRY: "Who did you take to the dance, Bob?"
5. GEORGE: "Why didn't you take the bus, Neal?"
6. HELEN: "How did you find out, Barbara?"
7. TOM: "What happened to your arm, Fred?"
8. BOB: "Who fixed the radio, Helen?"

Take the part of Speaker B. Report what was said.

1. TOM   "Where's your bike, Bill?"
   SPEAKER A I couldn't hear. Will you tell me what was said.
   SPEAKER B Tom asked Bill where his bike was.

Continue.

| Extra Drill 30.5 | **Indirect *Wh*- Questions** |

Take the part of Speaker A.

SPEAKER A

① *How are you?*

③ Yes, certainly.
   I asked you *how you were*.

SPEAKER B

② Excuse me./Pardon me.
   I didn't hear you.
   Would you repeat the question, please?

④ Oh. *I'm fine, thank you.*

1. How are you?   I'm fine, thank you.
2. What's your name?   My name's...
3. Where are you from?   I'm from...
4. What time is it?   It's 2:30 sharp.
5. What flight is Capt. Smith on?   He's on Flight 32.
6. Where's the gas truck?   It's down that way.
7. Who's that pretty girl over there?   That's the new flight instructor.
8. When do you want to refuel the 747?   Right now.
9. Where's the baggage cart?   It's coming now.
10. Where does the toolbox go?   Give it to me. I'll take it.

| Extra Drill 30.6 | Included *Wh-* Questions (After "I don't know") |

Take the part of Speaker B. Begin each reply with "I don't know."

SPEAKER A	SPEAKER B
1. Where's Bill?	I don't know where he is.
2. Who gave Mary the ring?	I don't know who gave it to her.
3. When did Mrs. Black leave?	....
4. Where did Tom buy his watch?	....
5. How did Henry feel?	....
6. Where did Barbara lose her money?	....
7. Why did Steve leave so early?	....
8. Where did Mr. Smith meet his wife?	....
9. What did he say?	....
10. Who took my book?	....

| Extra Drill 30.7 | Included *Wh-* Questions |

A. Take the part of Speaker B. Stress the question word.

SPEAKER A	SPEAKER B
1. When did the accident happen?	I don't know *when it happened.*
2. Where's Tom?	I've no idea *where he is.*
3. Who told you that?	I can't remember ....
4. How old is Mrs. Johnson?	I'm not sure ....
5. How far is it to the next town?	I don't know ....
6. What happenend to Bill?	I haven't heard ....
7. Is it getting late?	I've no idea ....
8. How far is it to Cedarville?	I can't tell you ....

B. Do the drill again. This time stress the word before the question word.

1. When did the accident happen? | I don't know *when it happened.*
2. Where's Tom? | I've no idea *where he is.*

Continue.

31 INDIRECT QUESTIONS: YES/NO QUESTIONS

> **Extra Drill 31.1**   Indirect Yes/No Questions with *if*

A. Report the questions that Miss Brown asked John. Use *if* as the subordinator.

MISS BROWN	REPORTER
1. "Can you see the blackboard?"	She asked him if he could see the blackboard.
2. "Do you know the answer?"	She asked him if he knew the answer.
3. "Did you study?"	....
4. "Did you hear me?"	....
5. "Do you understand the question?"	....
6. "Do you have a book?"	....

B. Report the questions that Mr. Farmer asked you (the reporter).

MR. FARMER	REPORTER
1. "Do you speak English?"	He asked me if I spoke English.
2. "Do you live with your parents?"	....
3. "Would you like to travel around the world?"	....
4. "Do you know how man learned to write?"	....
5. "Will you give a lecture to my students?"	....
6. "Do you know Dr. Ferguson?"	....

> **Extra Drill 31.2**   Indirect Yes/No Questions with *if*

A. Use *if* in the indirect questions.

1. "Can you go, Ted?" Tom asked.
   Tom asked Ted if he could go.

2. "May I take your picture?" Bob asked Lisa.
   ....

3. "Is that your book?" Bill asked me.
   ....

4. "Will you call Carlos?" I asked Tom.
   ....

5. "Must you leave, Mr. Wilson?" we asked.
   ....

6. "Should I go to the meeting?" I asked.
   ....

B. Use *whether* in the indirect questions.

1. "Are you comfortable, Mrs. Farmer?" I asked.
   I asked Mrs. Farmer whether she was comfortable.

2. "Would you like something to drink?" I asked him.
   ....

3. "Can you tell us, Mother?" we asked.
   ....

4. "Do you know June?" I asked Bob.
   ....

5. "Will you call me tomorrow?" June asked Barbara.
   ....

6. "Are you going to apply for the job?" Mrs. Bell asked her husband.
   ....

| Extra Drill 31.3 | **Indirect Yes/No Questions with *if*** |

Use the past perfect (*had* + past participle) in reporting these Yes/No questions. Use *if* as the subordinator.

1. "Have you met Mrs. Wilson?" I asked Mrs. Palmer.
   I asked Mrs. Palmer if she'd met Mrs. Wilson.

2. "Have you told anyone?" Tom asked Bob.
   ....

3. "Has Mr. Farmer arrived yet?" they asked me.
   ....

4. Tom asked his brother, "Have you decided to go?"
   ....

5. "Have you ever been to Brazil?" Mrs. Failor asked me.
   ....

6. "Have you ever heard of Dr. Ferguson?" Bob asked Jim.
   ....

7. "Have you seen my history book?" I asked Tom.
   ....

Extra Drill 31.4 — **Indirect Yes/No Questions with** *whether or not*

A. Report the questions that Mr. Fama asked his son, Tom. Use *whether...or not*.

MR. FAMA	REPORTER
1. "Can you go?"	He asked him whether he could go or not.
2. "Will you come?"	He asked him whether he'd come or not.
3. "Did you know it?"	....
4. "Have you finished?"	....
5. "Do you have to study?"	....
6. "Did you tell your mother?"	....

Repeat the exercise using *if...or not*.

B. Report the questions that Mr. Palmer asked Miss Thompson. Use *whether or not*.

MR. PALMER	REPORTER
1. "Do you want to apply for the job?"	He asked her whether or not she wanted to apply for the job.
2. "Do you have any experience?"	....
3. "Do you speak Spanish?"	....
4. "Have you studied science?"	....
5. "Can you type?"	....
6. "Would you be able to start work on Monday?"	....

Extra Drill 31.5 — **Included Yes/No Questions with** *whether...or not*

Answer the questions. Begin each response with "I'm sorry. I can't remember..." Use *whether...or not*.

SPEAKER A	SPEAKER B
1. Did you turn off the light?	I'm sorry. I can't remember whether I turned it off or not.
2. Did you close the windows?	....
3. Did you lock the car?	....
4. Did you turn off the stove?	....
5. Did you tell Mary?	....

6. Did you see Anne? ....
7. Did you return my book? ....
8. Did you invite Janet? ....

| Extra Drill 31.6 | Included Yes/No Questions with *if...or not* |

Answer the questions. Use *if...or not*.

SPEAKER A	SPEAKER B
1. Can you go?	I don't know if I can or not.
2. Have you met Mr. Jones?	I don't know if I have or not.
3. Will Tom be able to go?	....
4. Does Mary have enough money?	....
5. Should we tell Anne?	....
6. Is Helen going?	....
7. Is your father home?	....
8. Was that Dr. Smith?	....

Continue.

32 INDIRECT SPEECH: WITH IMPERATIVES

| Extra Drill 32.1 | Imperatives in Indirect Speech |

A. Report the directions that Miss Brown gave to her class. You are a student in the class.

MISS BROWN	REPORTER
1. "Repeat the dialog."	She asked us to repeat the dialog.
2. "Memorize the Basic Sentences."	She asked us to memorize the Basic Sentences.
3. "Repeat after me."	....
4. "Pronounce the words on page 19."	....
5. "Translate page 22."	....
6. "Write a composition."	....
7. "Do the exercises in Unit 2."	....

B. Report what Mr. White told his son to do. You are the son.

	MR. WHITE	REPORTER (MR. WHITE'S SON)
1.	"Wash the car."	He told me to wash to car.
2.	"Go to your room and study."	....
3.	"Put the car in the garage."	....
4.	"Practice your music lesson."	....
5.	"Be nice to your brother."	....
6.	"Clean up your room."	....
7.	"Be back by 11:00."	....

Extra Drill 32.2 — Imperatives in Indirect Speech (Negative)

Report what Mrs. Flower told her daughter Millie.

MRS. FLOWER	"Don't break any dishes."
TEACHER	What did Mrs. Flower tell Millie not to do?
REPORTER	She told her not to break any dishes.

Continue.

Extra Drill 32.3 — Imperatives in Indirect Speech

A. Report what Mr. Steel said to his secretary.

	MR. STEEL	REPORTER
1.	"Tell Mr. Brown to wait."	He asked her to tell Mr. Brown to wait.
2.	"Don't type the letter to Mr. Jones yet."	He told her ....
3.	"Open the mail."	....
4.	"Put the letters on my desk."	....
5.	"Don't worry about making a few mistakes."	....

B. Report what Officer Long, a policeman, said to Mr. Failor.

	CAPTAIN LONG	REPORTER
1.	"Don't park in front of the school."	He told him not to park in front of the school.
2.	"Park behind the school."	He told him ....
3.	"Pull over to the side of the road."	....
4.	"Stop."	....
5.	"Don't drive so fast."	....
6.	"Go ahead."	....
7.	"Be careful."	....

33 INDIRECT SPEECH: PRONOUN FORMS

Extra Drill 33.1   **Pronouns in Indirect Speech**

A. Report what Mr. Johnson said to you (the reporter).

	MR. JOHNSON	REPORTER
		(Begin with "He asked," or "He told," as appropriate.)
1.	"Can you speak Portuguese?"	He asked me if I could speak Portuguese.
2.	"How's your sister?"	....
3.	"Don't worry about it."	....
4.	"Your friend is waiting for you."	....
5.	"Where are you from?"	....
6.	"Where do you live?"	....

B. Report what Miss White said to you and your friend.

	MISS WHITE	REPORTER
1.	"Where are you going?"	She asked us where we were going.
2.	"Can I give you a ride?"	She asked us if ....
3.	"Where do you live?"	....
4.	"Put your books in the back seat."	....
5.	"Where did you learn English?"	....
6.	"I know your teacher."	....

| Extra Drill 33.2 | **Pronouns in Indirect Speech**

Jim, Bob, Pat, Helen and you (the reporter) are talking. Report what was said. Use pronoun forms for the indirect object and the subject of the clause.

REPORTER
(In reporting Yes/No questions, use *if* as the subordinator.)

1. Bob asks Lisa, "Should we tell Jim?"
   Bob asked her if they should tell Jim.

2. Jim asks you and Bob, "Should we take the girls to a movie?"
   Jim asked us if we should take the girls to a movie.

3. Lisa asks, Helen, "Do you think we should go?"
   ....

4. Bob asks you and Jim, "Do we have enough money?"
   ....

5. You ask Jim and Bob, "What movie should we go to?"
   ....

6. Helen asks you, "Do we have a test tomorrow?"
   ....

7. You say to Helen, "I don't think we do."
   ....

8. Jim asks all of you, "Should we drive or walk?"
   ....

9. You say to everyone, "I think we should walk.
   ....

10. Lisa says to everyone, "If we don't hurry, we'll be late for the movie."
    ....

34 INDIRECT SPEECH: ADVERBIALS OF TIME AND PLACE; VERBS *come/go* AND *bring/take*

Extra Drill 34.1 — *Here* and *there* in Indirect Speech

Change *there* to *here*. First listen to the conversation. Change *there* to *here* in Mr. Black's report of the conversation.

Mr. White and Mr. Black are talking on the telephone. It's Tuesday evening.

It's Wednesday in Mr. Black's office. Mr. Black reports the telephone conversation to Mr. Jones.

MR. BLACK

MR. WHITE	Can I meet you at *your office tomorrow*?	Mr. White asked if he could meet me *here today*.
MR. BLACK	I'll be *there* from two to four o'clock.	I said ....
MR. WHITE	I'll try to be *there* at 2:00.	He said ....
MR. BLACK	Mr. Foster can't get *there* before 2:30.	I told him ....
MR. WHITE	I'll see you and Mr. Foster *there* at 2:30 sharp.	He said ....

Extra Drill 34.2 — Time Adverbials in Indirect Speech

In reporting: Change *tomorrow* to *the next day*.
 Change *yesterday* to *the day before*.
 Change *last week* to *the week before*.

Mr. White made these statements to you (the reporter) on Monday. You are reporting them one week later. Use the past perfect when reporting the past tense verbs.

	MR. WHITE [Monday, July 7]	REPORTER [Monday, July 14]
1.	"I went to New York *last week*."	He told me he'd gone to New York *the week before*.
2.	"I'll do it *tomorrow*."	He told me he'd do it *the next day*.
3.	"I saw Tom *yesterday*."	....
4.	"I'm leaving *tomorrow*."	....
5.	"I'll send it to you *tomorrow*."	....
6.	"I wrote my lawyer *yesterday*."	....

7. "I'll call you *tomorrow*." ....
8. "I went to the doctor *last week*." ....
9. "I'll pay you *tomorrow*." ....
10. "I received the letter *last week*." ....

| Extra Drill 34.3 | **Time Adverbials in Indirect Speech** |

Choose the correct time word or expression in parentheses. The time words in brackets above the name of the speaker indicate the time or day when the speaker made a statement, and the time when it is being reported.

1. [Monday]
   MRS. FAILOR   "I can't tell you now."
   [Wednesday]
   REPORTER   Mrs. Failor said she couldn't tell me ....
                                                      (now, then, soon)

2. [Wednesday, May 10]
   MR. WHITE   "I saw Tom day before yesterday."
   [Friday, May 12]
   REPORTER   Mr. White said he'd seen Tom ....
                                     (in two days, on Monday, last week)

3. [Monday]
   MR. FARMER   "I promise you I'll do it today."
   [Friday]
   REPORTER   Mr. Farmer promised me he'd do it ....
                                    (today, the next day, that day)

4. [Tuesday]
   BARBARA   "I'm getting married tomorrow."
   [Saturday]
   REPORTER   Barbara told me she was getting married ....
                                (that day, the following day, in two days)

5. [Monday]
   MRS FAMA   "We'll give you our answer next week."
   [Wednesday]
   REPORTER   They said they'd give us their answer ....
                                       (next week, week after next)

6. [11:30 a.m., Thursday]
   MISS GREEN   "Mr. Foster called a few minutes ago."
   [3:00 p.m., Thursday]
   REPORTER   Miss Green said that Mr. Foster called ....
   (early this morning, before noon, at noon)

7. [Tuesday]
   HARRIET   "Margaret arrived yesterday."
   [Thursday]
   REPORTER   Harriet said that Margaret arrived ....
   (on Monday, the next day, on Tuesday)

8. [Monday]
   MRS. BROOKS   "I can't see you now."
   [Thursday]
   REPORTER   Mrs. Brooks told me she couldn't see me ....
   (the next day, now, then)

9. [Wednesday]
   JIM   "I'll return the money tomorrow."
   [Saturday]
   REPORTER   He told me he'd return the money ....
   (tomorrow, the following day, in two days)

Extra Drill 34.4 **Summary Drill: Reporting Speech**

The teacher will ask you questions. Look at the picture and then reply.

Examples:

TEACHER	STUDENT
Who's talking on the telephone?	Jean Watts is.
Who's Jean talking to?	Mrs. Drake.
What did Jean say to her?	She told her to wait just a minute. She said she would call Dr. Hunter.

Continue.

35 VERB + INFINITIVE

Extra Drill 35.1 — **Verb + Infinitive**

Substitute progressively.

	When do you plan to study?
prefer	....
expect	....
try	....
like	....
Why	....
need	....
send the package	....
want	....
did	....
promise	....
forget	....
decide	Why did you decide to send the package?

Extra Drill 35.2 — **Verb + Infinitive**

Substitute progressively.

	John wants to see the movie.
magazine	....
Past Tense	....
to buy	....
Yes/No Question	....
Henrietta	....
mystery story	....
decide	....
Affirmative Statement	....
to read	....
hope	....
Present Tense	....
plan	....
poem	Henrietta plans to read the poem.

| Extra Drill 35.3 | **Verb + Infinitive** |

Repeat these sentence parts to build up complete sentences.

1. 　　　　　...to swim
　　　　　...to learn to swim
　　　　　...to start to learn to swim
　When are you going to start to learn to swim?

2. 　　　　　...to play the piano
　　　　　...to learn to play the piano
　　　　　...to start to learn to play the piano
　When are you going to start to learn to play the piano?

3. 　　　　　...another foreign language
　　　　　...to speak another foreign language
　　　　　...to learn to speak another foreign language
　　　　　...to try to learn to speak another foreign language
　When are you going to try to learn to speak another foreign language?

| Extra Drill 35.4 | **Verb + Infinitive** |

Take the part of Speaker B and answer the questions using the cued words.

	SPEAKER A	SPEAKER B
1.	Does Carolyn want to visit France this spring? *(Austria)*	No, she wants to visit Austria.
2.	Should I start to plant the corn in April? *(in early May)*	No, you should start to plant it in early May.
3.	Does the medical society plan to have its annual meeting in Houston this year? *(Dallas)*	....
4.	Did Mrs. Bailey forget to cover the beans? *(spinach)*	....
5.	Have you decided to go in the fall? *(winter)*	....
6.	Will the electric company try to raise its rates before January 1? *(after January 1)*	....
7.	Did Warren try to learn to play the piano when he was young? *(the trumpet)*	....
8.	Has Mrs. Walker decided to begin to stock lawn furniture in his sporting goods store? *(bicycles)*	....

36 SPECIAL VERB EXPRESSIONS

Extra Drill 36.1 **Verb Expression** *be to*

Take the part of Speaker B and answer the questions. Use *be to* **and one of the alternatives that Speaker A gives.***

	SPEAKER A	SPEAKER B
1.	Do you know whether we're supposed to leave at nine or ten o'clock?	We're to leave at ten o'clock.
2.	Do you know whether we're supposed to begin this week or next week?	....
3.	Do you know whether I'm supposed to return this book to the teacher or to the library?	....
4.	Do you know whether I'm supposed to pick Shirley up at her office or at her house?	....
5.	Do you know whether I'm supposed to send this package first class or by parcel post?	....
6.	Do you know whether they're supposed to arrive at Union Station or Victoria Station?	....
7.	Do you know whether they're supposed to notify us by mail or by phone?	....
8.	Do you remember whether I'm supposed to take the car for a checkup at 10,000 miles or 12,000 miles?	....

*The tape always gives the last alternative.

Extra Drill 36.2 **Verb Expression** *be supposed to*

Look at the pictures and substitute in the sentence.

1.

You're not supposed *to cross the street* here.

2.

....

3.

4.

5.

6.

7.

| Extra Drill 36.3 | **Verb Expressions** *have to, used to, be about to* |

Repeat.

1. ...on the corner
   ...that little brown house on the corner
   ...to live in that little brown house on the corner
   They used to live in that little brown house on the corner.

2. ...when some friends came
   ...to leave the house when some friends came
   We were about to leave the house when some friends came.

3. ...any more dialogs
   ...to memorize any more dialogs
   ...we don't have to memorize any more dialogs
   I hope we don't have to memorize any more dialogs.

Extra Drill 36.4   Special Verb Expressions (With Indirect Speech)

Answer the questions.

What did Mr. Smith say?
He said the bus was about to leave.

What did the students say?
....

What did Mrs. DaSilva say?
....

What did Fred say?
....

What did Lisa say?
....

What did Jean Harris say?
....

What did the weatherman say?
....

What did Captain Morgan say?
....

37 ADJECTIVE + INFINITIVE

| Extra Drill 37.1 | **Adjective + Infinitive** |

Substitute progressively.

	I was anxious to meet them.
pleased	I was pleased to meet them.
delighted	. . . .
to see	. . . .
Present	. . . .
you	. . . .
happy	. . . .
to meet	. . . .
pleased	. . . .
to know	. . . .
glad	. . . .
to meet	I'm glad to meet you.

38 VERB OR ADJECTIVE + INFINITIVE: SHORT ANSWERS

| Extra Drill 38.1 | **Short Answers to Verb + Infinitive** |

Listen and repeat.

/gowiŋtə/
Are they *going to* cóme?
Why isn't she going to call us?
I wasn't going to say anything.

/gówiŋ tuw/
They're *góing to*.
She's going to.
I wasn't going to.

/hæftə/ - /hæstə/
They *have to* téll us.
Don't they have to see it?
She has to know about it.

/hǽf tuw/ - /hǽs tuw/
They *háve to*.
They don't have to.
She has to.

/wantə/
We *want to* gó with you.
They want to meet you.
I don't want to go.

/wánt tuw/
We *wánt to*.
They want to.
I don't want to.

71

| Extra Drill 38.2 | **Short Answers to Verb or Adjective + Infinitive** |

Speaker B: Answer Speaker A's question according to the statement of fact. Use past tense in the answers.

> **STATEMENT OF FACT**
> 1. I wanted to tell Jack.
> 2. Mary promised to help her brother today.
> 3. Helen was afraid to go with me in that little boat.
> 4. I was willing to pay for all the tickets.
> 5. Jack needed to go to the bank.
> 6. Mr. Watson had to sell his house.

SPEAKER A	SPEAKER B
1. Why did you tell Jack?	Because I wanted to.
2. Why's Mary helping her brother today?	....
3. Why didn't Helen go with you in that little boat?	....
4. Why did you pay for all the tickets?	....
5. Why did Jack go to the bank?	....
6. Why did Mr. Watson sell his house?	....

| Extra Drill 38.3 | **Negative Short Answers to Verb or Adjective + Infinitive** |

Speaker B: Answer Speaker A's question according to the statement of fact.

> **STATEMENT OF FACT**
> 1. I'm not ready to take the examination.
> 2. They're not able to attend the lectures.
> 3. Martha doesn't like to tell people about her personal problems.
> 4. We aren't supposed to memorize the dialog.
> 5. Dr. Guttag isn't ready to write up a report about his research.
> 6. Phil doesn't try to get good marks.

SPEAKER A	SPEAKER B
1. Why don't you take the examination?	Because I'm not ready to.
2. Why don't they attend the lectures?	....
3. Why doesn't Martha tell people about her personal problems?	....
4. Why don't you memorize the dialog?	....

5. Why doesn't Dr. Guttag write up a report about his research? ....
6. Why doesn't Phil get good marks? ....

39 INFINITIVE OF PURPOSE

| Extra Drill 39.1 | **Infinitive of Purpose**

Combine the two sentences into one sentence.

1. He called. He wanted to say he was sorry.
   He called to say he was sorry.

2. She stopped. She wanted to invite us to lunch.
   ....

3. They came. They wanted to tell us the good news.
   ....

4. Henry studied. He wanted to pass his exams.
   ....

5. We went early. We wanted to get a good seat.
   ....

6. Mr. and Mrs. Johnson came. They wanted to visit us.
   ....

7. I went to the store on the corner. I wanted to buy some bread.
   ....

8. We decided to go to the cafeteria. We wanted to have dinner.
   ....

9. Mrs. Brown came to the door. She wanted to borrow a cup of sugar.
   ....

10. I went to the post office. I wanted to mail a package.
    ....

40 VERB + GERUND

Extra Drill 40.1 **Verb + Gerund**

Change the sentences using the cued verb + a gerund.

1. He thinks I should go to another doctor. (recommend)
   He recommends going to another doctor.

2. I'm wondering whether I should wait until next year. (consider)
   I'm considering waiting until next year.

3. They didn't make a decision for nearly four weeks. (postpone)
   ....

4. He says he didn't throw away the notice. (deny)
   ....

5. The lawyer told us to have it checked by an expert. (advise)
   ....

6. Your job is also to clean the salad table at the end of the day. (include)
   ....

7. She might get her fingers burned. (risk)
   ....

8. Mr. Clark used to like to walk his dog in the mornings. (enjoy)
   ....

9. We don't like to have to pay a tax on food. (resent)
   ....

10. Yes, I did leave my car in the Whites' driveway. (admit)
    ....

41 PREPOSITION + GERUND

Extra Drill 41.1 **Verb or Preposition + Gerund**

Answer the question using a gerund.

1.

What did Amy recommend?
She recommended leaving early.

2.

What's Mel good at?
He's good at playing tennis.

3.

What's Bill interested in?
....

4.

What do the Parkers enjoy?
....

5.

What did Mr. Kelly postpone?
....

6.

What's Mrs. French excited about?
....

7.

What are the Russos sad about?
....

8.

What did Tom recommend?
....

9.

What's the lady in the first row worried about?
....

10.

What are Mr. and Mrs. Brown looking forward to?
....

| Extra Drill 41.2 | **Verb or Preposition + Gerund** |

Repeat.

1. ...late at night
   ...going to bed late at night
   ...early in the morning | and going to bed late at night
   ...get tired of getting up early in the morning | and going to bed late at night

   I sometimes get tired of getting up early in the morning | and going to bed late at night.

2. ...wild animals
   ...pictures of wild animals
   ...and taking pictures of wild animals
   ...going to Africa | and taking pictures of wild animals
   ...he told us about going to Africa | and taking pictures of wild animals

   In his lecture he told us about going to Africa and taking pictures of wild animals.

| Extra Drill 41.3 | **Short Answers to Verb or Preposition + Gerund** |

Speaker B: Answer the questions. Use short answers.

	SPEAKER A	SPEAKER B
1.	Do you recommend buying land in the country now?	No, I don't.
2.	Did Ron laugh about forgetting his car key?	No, ...
3.	Was Mr. Caldwell talking about going into the restaurant business?	Yes, ...
4.	Have the Thompsons put off buying a new car?	Yes, ...
5.	Were Don and Joyce McClure talking about going to Africa?	No, ...
6.	Would you consider going into dentistry?	No, ...
7.	Did he admit taking the watch?	Yes, ...
8.	Has your aunt finished planting her garden?	Yes, ...
9.	Was he successful in making new friends?	No, ...
10.	Do you believe in trying to do your best?	Yes, ...

| Extra Drill 41.4 | *It* **as Substitute for a Gerund** |

Speaker B: Answer the questions. Substitute the pronoun *it* for the gerund phrase.

	SPEAKER A	SPEAKER B
1.	Have you considered buying a new tent?	Yes, I've considered it.
2.	Are you excited about going back to your hometown?	No, I'm not excited about it.
3.	Do you advise swimming alone?	No, ...
4.	Are you tired of getting up early in the morning?	Yes, ...
5.	Do you enjoy playing chess?	Yes, ...
6.	Does Arthur like studying every night?	No, ...
7.	Are they considering attending the state university?	No, ...
8.	Have you ever thought about taking art lessons?	Yes, ...
9.	Did Professor Elliot give up smoking?	Yes, ...
10.	Will we ever get used to measuring in inches and feet?	Yes, ...

42 VERBS FOLLOWED BY EITHER GERUNDS OR INFINITIVES

| Extra Drill 42.1 | **Verb + Either Infinitive or Gerund** |

Substitute progressively.

Greg *started to study* foreign languages then.

studying ....
began ....
to study ....
intended ....
hated ....
preferred ....
studying ....
continued ....
to study ....
loved ....
studying Greg loved studying foreign languages then.

43 GERUNDS AND INFINITIVES AS SUBJECTS AND COMPLEMENTS

| Extra Drill 43.1 | **Gerunds as Complement of** *be* |

Change the sentences. Use gerunds.

1. Mr. Black teaches.
   His job's teaching.

2. Mrs. Jones teaches English.
   Her job's teaching English.

3. She teaches French and Spanish.
   ....

4. He teaches mathematics and astronomy.
   ....

5. Mr. Wells fixes things.
   ....

6. Mrs. Long makes clothes.
   ....

7. Mrs. White nurses.
   ....

8. Mr. Thomas repairs watches.
   ....

9. Bob Clark washes dishes in a restaurant.
   ....

10. Mrs. Burke does housework.
    ....

11. Mrs. Nicely washes and irons clothes.
    ....

12. Miss Neal takes care of children.
    ....

Extra Drill 43.2 — Negative Gerund as Subject of Sentence

Change the sentences. Use a negative gerund phrase as subject; use pronouns for the object of the gerund.

1. Jeffrey doesn't study for his exams.
   Not studying for them is a serious mistake.

2. Carla didn't get an extra apartment key.
   Not getting one was a serious mistake.

3. Walt didn't have his driver's license with him.
   ....

4. Mr. Finch didn't put any money in the parking meter.
   ....

5. He didn't put the terms of the agreement in writing.
   ....

6. They didn't take their car in for service regularly.
   ....

7. Ginny doesn't proofread her letters.
   ....

8. Jim didn't replace the needle of his record player.
   ....

9. The Corbetts don't have enough insurance on their house.
   ....

10. They don't require identification to get in the factory.
    ....

44 *It* and *there* AS SENTENCE SUBJECTS

Extra Drill 44.1   *It* as Subject; Infinitive in Complement

Change the sentences. Use *it* as subject.

1. To dance is fun.
   It's fun to dance.

2. To drive a car well takes experience.
   It takes experience to drive a car well.

3. To choose a good school is important.
   ....

4. To drive fast when it's raining is not a good idea.
   ....

5. To make noise when other students are studying is impolite.
   ....

6. To harvest crops at the right time is important.
   ....

7. To build a house all by yourself takes a long time.
   ....

8. To increase the world's food supply would not be difficult.
   ....

9. To be right all the time is impossible.
   ....

10. To be a good doctor takes a great deal of education and experience.
    ....

Extra Drill 44.2   **Gerund as Subject**

Answer the questions using a gerund as subject. Use *a lot of* or *very* as an intensifier.

	SPEAKER A	SPEAKER B
1.	Is it fun to swim?	Yes, swimming's a lot of fun.
2.	Is it hard to ride a horse?	No, riding a horse isn't very hard.
3.	Is it hard to give the right answer every time?	Yes, ...
4.	Is it pleasant to sit in front of a fire?	Yes, ...
5.	Is it easy to build a fire?	No, ...

6. Does it usually take a long time to learn a foreign language well?   Yes, ...
7. Is it always fun to picnic by the river?   Yes, ...
8. Is it polite to interrupt people when they're speaking?   No, ...
9. Does it take experience to teach your native language to someone?   Yes, ...
10. Does it give you satisfaction to camp in the woods?   Yes, ...
11. Does it make you tired to drive at night?   No, ...
12. Is it simple to camp out in the woods overnight?   No, ...

| Extra Drill 44.3 | *There* as Subject |

Repeat each sentence and then form another sentence using the cued words.

1. Several children were on the playground. *(squirrels)*
   Several children were on the playground. There were several squirrels there, too.
2. A good play will be at the theater next week. *(the week after next)*
   A good play will be at the theater next week. There will be a good play there the week after next, too.
3. A good campground is right over there. *(a fine lake)*
   ....
4. A new office building is on Second Street. *(drugstore)*
   ....
5. Some clean shirts are in the top drawer. *(second drawer)*
   ....
6. A policeman was on the corner. *(several college students)*
   ....
7. Some fine camping equipment was in the store window. *(skiing equipment)*
   ....
8. Fifteen or twenty cows are in the barn. *(pasture)*
   ....
9. Some children will be at tonight's play. *(adults)*
   ....
10. A lot of water is in the garage. *(basement)*
    ....

Extra Drill 44.4 — *There* as Subject; Gerund in Complement

Change the sentences. Use *there* in subject position.

1. A baby was crying in the bedroom.
   There was a baby crying in the bedroom.

2. A lot of people were running in the street.
   There were a lot of people running in the street.

3. Several firemen were hurrying into the burning house.
   There were several firemen hurrying into the burning house.

4. Some men were arguing about the accident.
   ....

5. A radio was playing in the next room.
   ....

6. A man was attempting to steal money from the bank.
   ....

7. Some water was boiling on the stove.
   ....

8. Several couples were dancing to the music.
   ....

9. Thousands of colorful fish were swimming near our boat.
   ....

10. A lot of people were dancing and singing in the streets.
    ....

11. Several other people were waiting at the restaurant.
    ....

12. A long black car was coming toward us.
    ....

13. Several people were hurrying to catch the bus.
    ....

14. Quite a few people were waiting for the airplane to come in.
    ....

15. A lot of black smoke was coming from the factory.
    ....

45 NOMINAL PHRASES

Extra Drill 45.1 Nominal Phrases (Stress)

Repeat these phrases paying particular attention to the stress.

wool coat	cotton dress	spring flowers
gold ring	silver ring	fall weather
grass skirt	plastic spoon	gold necklace
brick house	apple pie	fruit cocktail
straw roof	paper plate	clam chowder
peach pie	corner store	log cabin
crab soup	summer rain	wool clothing
stone bridge	winter snow	silk stockings

Extra Drill 45.2 Adjective + Nominal Phrase (Stress)

Repeat these phrases and sentences.

blue cotton dress	She bought a blue cotton dress.
good lettuce salad	We had a good lettuce salad.
old silver watch	He carries an old silver watch.
big winter snow	We had a big winter snow.

Extra Drill 45.3 Nominal Phrases

Substitute progressively.

	She has a cotton sweater.
nylon	She has a nylon sweater.
Past Tense	....
bought	....
robe	....
silk	....
Yes/No Question	....
suit	....

Negative Statement	She didn't buy a silk suit.
dacron	....
wool	....
want	....
hat	....
Negative Question	....
straw	....
Affirmative Statement	....
get	She got a straw hat.

Extra Drill 45.4	**Nominal Phrases**

Repeat the nominal phrase in parentheses. Then answer the question.

1. Doesn't that house have an interesting straw roof? *(brick chimney)*
   Yes, and it has an interesting brick chimney too.

2. Didn't he eat all the fruit cocktail? *(apple pie)*
   Yes, and he ate all the apple pie too.

3. Didn't we have a lot of winter snow last year? *(spring rain)*
   ....

4. Wasn't she wearing a lovely silk blouse? *(straw hat)*
   ....

5. Isn't that the best place to get clam chowder? *(crab soup)*
   ....

6. Didn't you buy your gold necklace there? *(silver ring)*
   ....

7. Doesn't she hate to use paper plates? *(plastic spoons)*
   ....

8. Don't you enjoy the spring flowers in this region? *(autumn leaves)*
   ....

9. Isn't there a little stone bridge in the park? *(log cabin)*
   ....

10. Aren't they getting short of lead pipe? *(copper wire)*
    ....

| Extra Drill 45.5 | **Nominal Phrases (without Sentence Stress)** |

When another word has the sentence stress, the strong stress of the nominal phrase is reduced. Listen to the sentences and then repeat them.

The lettuce salad was good.

The wool coat's pretty.

The toy soldiers were broken.

The spring flowers are beautiful.

The corner store was closed.

| Extra Drill 45.6 | **Adjective + Nominal Phrase (Stress)** |

Substitute.

She had *some old brown leather shoes.*
     a new blue cotton dress
     an old green silk umbrella
     a new yellow summer dress
     an old black winter coat
     a little blue silk purse

| Extra Drill 45.7 | **Nominal Phrases (with Contrast Stress)** |

For contrast or emphasis, the noun modifier may have the strong stress. Listen to the question, and then, using the cue, form a sentence with contrast stress on the pre-modifying noun.

1. Don't you live in a stone house? *(brick house)*
   No, I live in a brick house, not a stone one.

2. Wasn't she wearing a wool skirt last night? *(cotton skirt)*
   No, she was wearing a cotton skirt, not a wool one.

3. Doesn't he collect gold coins? *(silver coins)*
   ....

4. Isn't she looking for a fall dress? *(winter dress)*
   ....

5. Doesn't a leather belt come with those slacks? *(plastic belt)*
   ....

6. Didn't you order a chocolate pie? *(lemon pie)*
   . . . .

7. Wouldn't they look best in a wooden vase? *(glass vase)*
   . . . .

8. Didn't he bring the plastic cups? *(china cups)*
   . . . .

9. Doesn't this boat have a metal bottom? *(wood bottom)*
   . . . .

10. Didn't they play at the evening concert? *(afternoon concert)*
    . . . .

46 NOUN COMPOUNDS

Extra Drill 46.1   Noun Compounds (Stress)

Substitute the noun compounds.

How large is the *living room?*
        dining room
        bedroom
        laundry room
        bathroom
        furnace room

Extra Drill 46.2   Noun Compounds Having Gerunds (Stress)

Repeat these noun compounds.

frying pan	wrapping paper
carving knife	drinking water
shaving cream	spending money
swimming pool	swimming party
drinking cup	filling station
sleeping bag	serving platter
walking shoes	drawing paper

| Extra Drill 46.3 | **Noun Compounds Having Gerunds (Stress)** |

Combine the two sentences into one sentence.

1. His hiking shoes were new. He almost wore them out.
   He almost wore out his new hiking shoes.
2. She needs some wrapping paper. It must be very strong.
   She needs some very strong wrapping paper.
3. I'll bring my sleeping bag. It's very warm.
   ....
4. They went on a fishing trip. It was quite long.
   ....
5. All the serving dishes were dirty. I had to wash them.
   ....
6. Our washing machine is old. We have to get rid of it.
   ....
7. This drinking water is delicious. I'm going to have some more.
   ....
8. The driving lesson was difficult. She had to practice it again.
   ....
9. The house had a dining room. It was huge.
   ....
10. Miss Green's getting a typing table. It's green.
    ....

| Extra Drill 46.4 | **Noun Compounds (without Sentence Stress)** |

In the sentences under (b), the last word has the sentence stress, and the strong stress of the noun compound is reduced. First listen to the sentences and then repeat them. Emphasize the primary stress in each sentence.

	(a)	(b)
1.	It's a big frying pan.	The frying pan's big.
2.	They're good hiking shoes.	The hiking shoes are good.
3.	It was a nice farm house.	....
4.	It was a red fire engine.	....
5.	It's a small dining room.	....

Extra Drill 46.5   **Noun Compounds (without Sentence Stress)**

Use the noun compound of the first sentence; add it to the second sentence.

1. She finished her housework. It's all done.
   Her housework's all done.

2. I've packed my suitcases. They're ready now.
   My suitcases are ready now.

3. Have you tried their seafood? It's wonderful.
   ....

4. He made her a dollhouse. It was for her birthday.
   ....

5. I found your notebook. It's in the car.
   ....

6. Please get the sugar bowl. It's on the top shelf.
   ....

7. I like this orange juice. It's frozen.
   ....

8. She couldn't find her dessert spoon. It was under her napkin.
   ....

Extra Drill 46.6   **Noun Compounds**

Speaker A asks questions. Speaker B replies in terms of the statement of fact.

> STATEMENT OF FACT
> 1. There were two *easy chairs* in the *living room*.
> 2. The *linen closet*'s in the *bedroom*.
> 3. The *washing machine*'s in the *laundry room*.
> 4. She carries *spending money* in her *pocketbook*.
> 5. I took my *hiking shoes* on the *camping trip*.
> 6. You can buy *shaving cream* at the *drugstore*.
> 7. I'm going to the *post office* to get some *postage stamps*.
> 8. That *shoe store* over there sells good *tennis shoes*.
> 9. You can get fresh *seafood* at the *seashore*.
> 10. There are five *English teachers* in our *high school*.
> 11. You can buy your *textbooks* at the *bookstore*.

	SPEAKER A	SPEAKER B
1.	Where were the easy chairs?	In the living room.
2.	Where's the linen closet?	In the bedroom.
3.	Is the washing machine in the kitchen?	. . . .
4.	What does she carry in her pocketbook?	. . . .

Continue.

47 COMPOUND NOUN PHRASES

Extra Drill 47.1   **Compound Noun Phrases with** *and*

Use the conjunction *and* to join the noun phrases. When the same modifier occurs more than once, use it only one time.

	TEACHER	STUDENT
1.	John - his brother	John and his brother
2.	my mother - my father	my mother and father
3.	some bread - some butter	. . . .
4.	my hat - my coat	. . . .
5.	John - Mary	. . . .
6.	my brother - your sister	. . . .
7.	your brother - your sister	. . . .
8.	the little boys - the little girls	. . . .
9.	a knife - a fork	. . . .
10.	my shoes - my socks	. . . .

Extra Drill 47.2   **Compound Noun Phrases with** *and*

Combine the sentences as in the examples.

1. John is coming.
   His brother is coming.
       John and his brother are coming.
2. He knows my mother.
   He knows my father.
       He knows my mother and father.

3. I'd like some bread.
   I'd like some butter.
   . . . .

4. Where's my hat?
   Where's my coat?
   . . . .

5. I need a knife.
   I need a fork.
   . . . .

6. The salt's on the table.
   The pepper's on the table.
   . . . .

7. My book's on the table.
   Your pen's on the table.
   . . . .

8. Some little boys were playing.
   Some little girls were playing.
   . . . .

| Extra Drill 47.3 | **Compound Noun Phrases with** *or* |

Combine the two elements with *or*.

	TEACHER	STUDENT
1.	tea - coffee	tea or cóffee
2.	Mrs. Smith - Mrs. Johnson	Mrs. Smith or Mrs. Johnson
3.	peas - carrots	. . . .
4.	Spain - Italy	. . . .
5.	potatoes - rice	. . . .
6.	Tom - Henry	. . . .
7.	ice cream - cake	. . . .
8.	tóy stŏre - tóy stòre	. . . .

Extra Drill 47.4   **Noun Phrases with *or* in Alternative Questions**

Listen to the two questions and then form one question as in the models.

1. Would you like tea?
   Would you like coffee?
       Would you like tea or coffee?

2. Did you order peas? Did you order carrots?
       Did you order peas or carrots?

3. Did you invite Mrs. Smith?
   Did you invite Mrs. Johnson?
   . . . .

4. Are they going to Spain?
   Are they going to Italy?
   . . . .

5. Would you like potatoes?
   Would you like rice?
   . . . .

6. Did Tom call his father?
   Did he call his mother?
   . . . .

7. Would you like ice cream?
   Would you like cake?
   . . . .

8. Did you borrow my sweater?
   Did you borrow my jacket?
   . . . .

Extra Drill 47.5   **Noun Phrases with *or* in Unlimited Choice**

If choices are not limited, a rising intonation is used. Listen, then repeat.

1. Would you like an apple or an orange?
2. Are they going to Chile or Peru?
3. Would you like a book or a magazine?
4. Would you like orange juice or tomato juice?
5. May I offer you some meat or potatoes?
6. Have you asked John or Bill?

| Extra Drill 47.6 | **Compound Noun Phrases with More Than Two Items** |

Answer the questions with complete sentences, using all the expressions in one of the lists of words given below.

two red pencils   a pound of rice   orange juice
a fountain pen   a dozen eggs   bacon and eggs
a notebook   a head of lettuce   buttered toast
some notebook paper   a quart of milk   a cup of coffee

John   a cup of soup   laughing   Barbara
Mary   a cheese sandwich   singing   Jean
Helen   a glass of milk   dancing   Harriet
          playing   Elsie

1. What does Tom always have for breakfast? ....
2. What school supplies did John buy? ....
3. What are the names of Mrs. Jones' daughters? ....
4. What did Mrs. Smith buy at the grocery store? ....
5. What did Helen have for lunch. ....
6. What were the children doing outside? ....
7. Who's coming to the party? ....

| Extra Drill 47.7 | *Both...and* **in Compound Noun Phrases** |

Speaker A asks questions. Speaker B replies in terms of the statement of fact. Use *both...and* **in your reply.**

STATEMENT OF FACT

1. John's coming. His brother's coming, too.
2. I know his mother. I know his father, too.
3. Coffee's a popular drink. Tea's also a popular drink.
4. Tom wants to be an engineer. Hank wants to be an engineer, too.
5. Jane hopes to be a nurse. Nancy hopes to be a nurse also.
6. Helen's a good cook. Barbara's also a good cook.
7. His wife is very proud of him. His daughter's very proud of him, too.
8. They had a radio. They had a television set, too.
9. He speaks Spanish. He also speaks Portuguese.
10. He's a lawyer. He's also a doctor.
11. Dr. Smith is a famous astronomer. His sister's also a famous astronomer, too.

1. Is John coming?   Yes, both John and his brother are coming.
2. Do you know his mother?   Yes, I know both his mother and father.
3. Is coffee a popular drink?   ....
4. Does Tom want to be an engineer?   ....
5. Does Jane hope to be a nurse?   ....
6. Is Helen a good cook?   ....
7. Is his wife very proud of him?   ....
8. Did they have a radio?   ....
9. Does he speak Spanish?   ....
10. Is he a lawyer?   ....
11. Is Dr. Smith a famous astronomer?   ....

48 CONJUNCTIONS WITH OTHER STRUCTURES

Extra Drill 48.1   Practices Joined with *and*

Combine the sentences using *and* to join the predicates.

1. We bought a house on Thursday.
   We moved in on Friday.
       We bought a house on Thursday and moved in on Friday.

2. George and Mary met in March.
   George and Mary got married in September.
       George and Mary met in March and got married in September.

3. The men caught some fish.
   The men cooked them for dinner.
   ....

4. I saw Harriet.
   I told her the good news.
   ....

5. She cleans.
   She cooks.
   She does the laundry.
   ....

6. We went on a picnic.
   We had a good time.
   ....

7. She saw me.
   She waved.
   ....

8. The children were laughing.
   The children were playing.
   The children were having a good time.
   ....

9. He asked me to sit down.
   He asked me to wait.
   ....

10. He came in.
    He sat down.
    He began to tell a story.
    ....

49 THE CONJUNCTION *but*

Extra Drill 49.1   **Noun Phrases Joined with *but* (Stress)**

Form noun phrases joined with *but...not*.

	TEACHER	STUDENT
1.	milk - coffee	milk, but not coffee
2.	John - Mary	John, but not Mary
3.	rice - potatoes	....
4.	vegetables - meat	....
5.	oranges and lemons - grapefruit	....
6.	Japan - Korea	....
7.	Mr. Smith - Mrs. Smith	....
8.	basketball - baseball	....

Extra Drill 49.2   **Noun Phrases Joined with *but***

Combine the sentences using *but not* to join noun phrases.

1. He likes milk.
   He doesn't like coffee.
   He likes milk, but not coffee.
2. I asked John.
   I didn't ask Mary.
   I asked John, but not Mary.
3. He eats rice.
   He doesn't eat potatoes.
   ....
4. They eat vegetables.
   They don't eat meat.
   ....
5. They grow oranges and lemons.
   They don't grow grapefruit.
   ....
6. I've visited Japan.
   I haven't visited Korea.
   ....
7. I know Mr. Smith.
   I don't know Mrs. Smith.
   ....
8. He plays basketball.
   He doesn't play baseball.
   ....

| Extra Drill 49.3 | Conjunctions with *but* |

Answer the questions with a sentence having *but*. Follow the models.

SPEAKER A | SPEAKER B
1. Was he big and strong? | He was big, but not strong.
2. Do you like Mary and her brother? | I like Mary, but not her brother.
3. Did he tell his father and his mother? | ....
4. Is George's uncle big and fat? | ....
5. Is her hair dark and long? | ....
6. Was the course interesting and easy? | ....
7. Does the baby like milk and cereal? | ....
8. Did you read the play and the novel? | ....
9. Is he well-known in New York and Paris? | ....
10. Was news of the accident in the newspaper and on the radio? | ....

50 SPECIAL NOUNS IN REFERENCE TO NUMBER

| Extra Drill 50.1 | Special Nouns |

Read the responses filling *is* or *are* in the blanks.

1. What did he say about the crowd?
   He said the crowd *is* leaving the parking lot.
2. What did he say is on the ground?
   He said a number of new boards *are* on the ground.
3. Did anyone expect that?
   No, the news .... a surprise to everyone.
4. Do they have many industries in the Netherlands?
   Yes, the Netherlands .... an important nation.
5. Do they have many telephones there?
   Yes, the number of telephones in that city .... increasing rapidly.
6. What's all the noise about?
   The people .... afraid of the storm.

7. Are their weapons primitive?
   Yes, the bow and arrow .... their most advanced weapon.
8. Do her in-laws live around here?
   No, her husband's family .... in Switzerland.

51 ADJECTIVES USED AS NOMINALS

| Extra Drill 51.1 | **Adjectives Used as Nominals**

Answer the questions using the cued adjectives.

1. Do poor people have many problems? *(rich)*
   Yes, and the rich have many problems too.
2. Are exotic things in style now? *(familiar)*
   Yes, and the familiar is in style now too.
3. Are successful people resented? *(clever)*
   ....
4. Are relative things hard to define? *(eternal)*
   ....
5. Do foolish people make mistakes? *(sensible)*
   ....
6. Were the hungry people taken care of right away? *(sick)*
   ....
7. Can he do difficult things? *(impossible)*
   ....
8. Do famous people get their names in the newspaper? *(bad)*
   ....

52 APPOSITIVES

Extra Drill 52.1 — **Appositives**

Substitute the noun phrases.

He introduced me to his friend, *a famous scientist.*
                      Bobby Simpson
                      the Ambassador from Peru
                      a young professor
                      a designer from Italy
                      a German archaeologist

Extra Drill 52.2 — **Appositives (Intonation)**

Substitute the noun phrases in Parts A, B and C. Pay particular attention to the intonation.

A. Patricia Wóod, *a girl in my árt class,* told me she wanted to méet you.
              the famous artist
              the clothes designer
              a neighbor of mine

B. Is that *Dr. Smíth*, the famous *anthropólogist?*

    John Glenn   astronaut
    Fran Walker   dancer
    Ms. Anita Crawford marine biologist
    George Barnes   tax accountant
    Rick Frey   scuba diver
    Tim Welch   world traveler
    Carol Nauss   movie critic

C. I'd like you to meet an old friend of mine, *Dave Nórdstrom.*
                                      Joan Mandel
                                      Keith Harmon
                                      Neal Fleming

| Extra Drill 52.3 | **Appositives** |

Complete the unfinished sentence with a noun phrase and an appositive.

1. The telephone was his invention.
   Alexander Graham Bell is famous for *his invention, the telephone.*
2. Jim Nash was an old friend of his.
   He asked me to meet *Jim Nash, an old friend of his.*
3. *The Old Man and the Sea* is a famous short story.
   Ernest Hemingway wrote ....
4. Frank Lloyd Wright was a well-known architect.
   That building was designed by .....
5. Neil Armstrong was the first man to step on the moon.
   Everybody has heard of ....
6. *A Tale of Two Cities* is a famous novel.
   ..... was written by Charles Dickens.
7. *Fire and Ice* is a well-known poem.
   .... was written by Robert Frost.
8. Albany is the capital of New York State.
   Have you ever heard of ....?
9. Echo Lake is one the the most beautiful lakes in the world.
   We always camp near ....

| Extra Drill 52.4 | **Appositives (with No Pause)** |

Change the form of the appositives as shown in the examples.

	TEACHER	STUDENT
1.	June, his sister, ...	his sister June
2.	Bill, my brother, ...	my brother Bill
3.	John, our friend, ...	....
4.	Lawrence, his uncle, ...	....
5.	Mary, my aunt, ...	....
6.	Jane, her daughter, ...	....
7.	Tom, their son, ...	....

Extra Drill 52.5 — Appositives

Speaker A asks questions. Speaker B answers the questions in terms of the statement of fact.

STATEMENT OF FACT

1. My sister Jane said she'd help us.
2. My brother Bill said he'd write us.
3. Our friend John told us all about it.
4. His uncle Lawrence comes every Tuesday.
5. My aunt Mary is like a second mother.
6. Her daughter Jane is a very good student.
7. Their son Tom is away at school now.

	SPEAKER A	SPEAKER B
1.	Who said she'd help us?	My sister Jane did.
2.	Who said he'd write us?	My brother Bill did.
3.	....	....
4.	....	....
5.	....	....
6.	....	....
7.	....	....

53 INFINITIVES AND GERUNDS WITH DIFFERENT MEANINGS AFTER CERTAIN VERBS

Extra Drill 53.1 — *Stop* + Infinitive of Purpose

John was going downtown. He stopped at my house.

Substitute.

He stopped *to borrow some money.*
        to have something to eat with us
        to fix my radio for me
        to invite us to go for a ride
        to look at my mother's garden
        to tell us about the letter he'd received

Extra Drill 53.2   *Stop* + **Gerund**

The doctor gave Mr. Smith some advice.

Substitute:

Dr. Hunter told Mr. Smith to stop *smoking*.
He also told him to stop ....

Extra Drill 53.3   *Remember* + **Infinitive**

Dr. Hunter is thinking of things he mustn't forget to do.

Substitute:

He said to himself, "I must remember *to call the hospital*."
                 "I also must remember ...."

| **Extra Drill 53.4** | *Remember* + **Gerund** |

John O'Brien remembers a lot about his childhood. He tells about things he did when he was six years old.

1. Did you pull your sister's hair? *(Yes)*
   Yes, I remember pulling my sister's hair.
2. Did you run away from home? *(No)*
   No, I don't remember running away from home.
3. Did you have a party for your sixth birthday? *(Yes)*
   ....
4. Did you eat hot dogs a lot? *(Yes)*
   ....
5. Did you like to climb trees? *(Yes)*
   ....
6. Did you fight with your older brother? *(No)*
   ....
7. Did you go fishing with your father? *(Yes)*
   ....
8. Did you break any windows? *(No)*
   ....
9. Did you play in the mud? *(Yes)*
   ....
10. Did you drink coffee at dinner? *(No)*
    ....
11. Did you go shopping with your mother? *(Yes)*
    ....
12. Did you sit next to a cute girl in first grade? *(Yes)*
    ....

54 COMPOUND MODIFIERS USING NUMBERS

Extra Drill 54.1 **Stress of Compound Modifiers Using Numbers**

Form compound modifiers from the cues as in the examples.

CUE

1. a house with six rooms — a six-room house
2. a trip that takes two years — a two-year trip
3. a lecture that takes three hours — ....
4. a family with two cars — ....
5. a house with three bedrooms — ....
6. an exam that takes two hours — ....
7. a letter with six pages — ....
8. a limit of two years — ....
9. a poem with two lines — ....
10. a guarantee of one year — ....
11. an adventure that lasts two days — ....
12. a job that takes two hours — ....
13. an assignment that takes two days — ....
14. a guitar that costs fifty dollars — ....
15. a hospital with fifty beds — ....
16. a hotel with six hundred rooms — ....
17. a program of two days — ....
18. a sightseeing trip of two hours — ....
19. a textbook with five hundred pages — ....
20. a car that holds six passengers — ....

| **Extra Drill 54.2** | **Compound Modifiers Using Numbers** |

Form a sentence with a compound modifier using a number.

1. Their house has a living room, dining room, kitchen and two bedrooms. How big is it? It's a five-room house.
2. They left Monday morning and came back Friday night. How long was their trip? It was a five-day trip.
3. The test started at 9 a.m. and was over at noon. How long was it?
   ....
4. He started the job yesterday and finished today. How long was the job?
   ....
5. I work on the tenth floor but there are fourteen floors above me. How high is this office building?
   ....
6. She's on page 375 and has one hundred more pages to read. How long is the book she's reading?
   ....
7. He started at two p.m. and didn't finish until four. How long was his lecture today?
   ....
8. The war lasted from March until June. How long was it?
   ....

55 NOUN PHRASE + INFINITIVE

| **Extra Drill 55.1** | **Noun Phrase (Gerund) + Infinitive Modifier** |

Substitute:

Does she have any *sewing* to do?
              washing
              cleaning
              ironing
              mending
              baking
              cooking
              shopping

| Extra Drill 55.2 | **Noun Phrase + Infinitive Modifier** |

A. Listen to these sentences.

1. Would you like *something to eat?*
2. I'm hungry. I haven't had *anything to eat* all day.
3. I don't think that boy gets *enough to eat.*
4. We didn't have *much to eat* all day.
5. I think he's had *too much to drink.*
6. I ate the bread, but there was *nothing else to eat.*
7. She had *nothing to say* about it.

B. Answer the questions with "There was nothing" and an infinitive.

1. Why did you come home early? *(do)*
   There was nothing to do so I came home early.
2. Why did they leave the party? *(eat)*
   There was nothing to eat so they left the party.
3. Why didn't he stay at the museum? *(see)*
   ....
4. Why did she keep quiet? *(say)*
   ....
5. Why didn't you like the sale? *(buy)*
   ....
6. Why did the teacher hand the papers back right away? *(correct)*
   ....

C. Answer the questions with "something else" and an infinitive.

1. Have you eaten the sandwich?
   Yes, but I have something else to eat too.
2. Has she ironed the shirts?
   Yes, but she has something else to iron too.
3. Have you cleaned the hunting knife?
   ....
4. Has the doctor checked their temperatures?
   ....
5. Has he written the introduction?
   ....
6. Have we paid the electric bill?
   ....

| Extra Drill 55.3 | **Noun Phrase + Infinitive Modifier** |

Complete the unfinished sentence using the information given.

1. Dr. Smith *gives lectures.*
   He has *a lecture to give this afternoon.*
2. Mr. Hoffman *attends* a lot of *meetings.*
   He has *a meeting to attend this afternoon.*
3. Mr. White *does* a lot of *work.*
   He has some ....
4. Dr. Brown *writes* a lot of *reports.*
   He has ....
5. Mr. Green *makes* a lot of *important telephone calls.*
   He has an ....
6. Mr. Green's secretary *types* a lot of *letters.*
   She has several ....
7. Mr. Clark *gives* a lot of *important speeches.*
   He has an ....
8. Dr. Wall *sees* a lot of *patients.*
   He has six ....

| Extra Drill 55.4 | **Noun Phrase + Infinitive Modifier** |

Repeat the sentences paying particular attention to the sentence stress.

1. He has a two-hour lécture to give.
2. He has a two-page repórt to write.
3. He has a two-day cónference to attend.
4. He has a one-hour spéech to give.
5. He has a two-hour méeting to attend.
6. He has a three-day prógram to organize.
7. He has a ten-minute tápe to make.

56 PARTICIPLES AS NOUN MODIFIERS: -ing FORM

| Extra Drill 56.1 | -ing **Participles as Noun Modifiers** |

Repeat the phrases and sentences.

running water   These houses have no running water.
following example   Please listen to the following example.
approaching storm   We watched the approaching storm.
talking doll   Mary's best present was a talking doll.

| Extra Drill 56.2 | -ing **Participles as Noun Modifiers** |

Answer the questions using the cued noun phrase.

1. Do these houses have electricity? (running water)
   Yes, they do. But they don't have any running water.
2. Did they see the coast? (approaching storm)
   Yes, they did. But they didn't see the approaching storm.
3. Did Mary get the dollhouse she wanted? (talking doll)
   ....
4. Did the doctor give you medicine for your sore foot? (aching back)
   ....
5. Are there any teenagers in the class? (working mothers)
   ....
6. Did he get out of the way of the truck? (falling tree)
   ....
7. Do you like to interview the players? (losing team)
   ....
8. Can you hear the fire whistle in this room? (barking dogs)
   ....

| Extra Drill 56.3 | **Contrasting Stress with -*ing* Modifiers** |

Repeat the phrases and sentences.

NOUN PHRASE	NOUN COMPOUND
bôiling wáter	drínking wàter
vîsiting núrse	vísiting hòurs
wâlking dóll	wálking shòes

1. I needed some bôiling wáter.   I needed some drínking wàter.
2. Who are the vîsiting núrses?   When are the vísiting hòurs?
3. Susan got a wâlking dóll.   Susan got some wálking shòes.

| Extra Drill 56.4 | **-*ing* Participle Phrase as Noun Modifier** |

Say the sentence again, omitting the italicized words.

1. The girl *who was* missing since yesterday was found.
   The girl missing since yesterday was found.
2. The people *who were* returning from Europe all had to take the boat.
   ....
3. Do you know the man *who's* running after the bus?
   ....
4. The plane *that's* circling the airport seems to be in trouble.
   ....
5. Do you know the people *who are* picnicking by the river?
   ....
6. The people *who were* dancing in the streets seemed to be very happy.
   ....
7. Do you know the man *who's* standing over there?
   ....
8. The lady *who's* talking now is Mrs. Failor.
   ....

Extra Drill 56.5   *-ing* **Participle Modifiers without Object or Complement**

Form noun phrases from the cues using *-ing* participles.

CUES

1. water which is boiling — boiling water
2. customers who are paying by the month — customers paying by the month
3. a building which is burning — ....
4. a student who is beginning — ....
5. students who are beginning this year — ....
6. students who are failing in geography — ....
7. a country which is developing — ....
8. ice which is melting in the street — ....
9. snow which is melting — ....
10. the girl who's amusing — ....
11. the girl who's amusing her friends — ....
12. the army which is attacking us — ....
13. the army which is attacking — ....
14. the boys who are arguing outside — ....
15. the men who are running in the streets — ....

Extra Drill 56.6 **-ing Participle Modifier—from a Simple Present Verb Form**

Form noun phrases from the cues.

CUES

1. the example that follows — the following example
2. an area that surrounds the lake — an area surrounding the lake
3. a problem that continues — ....
4. the lesson that follows this one — ....
5. a dictionary that pronounces — ....
6. a wall that protects — ....
7. a customer who pays — ....
8. a person who thinks — ....
9. birds which migrate — ....
10. a glass door that slides — ....

57 -ing FORMS AS TRUE ADJECTIVES

Extra Drill 57.1 **-ing Participles as True Adjectives**

Answer the questions.

SPEAKER A — SPEAKER B

1. Do you think she's an amusing child? — Yes. I think she's very amusing.
2. Did you think it was a boring program? — Yes, I thought it was very boring.
3. Did you see an exciting movie? — ....
4. Did you have a satisfying experience? — ....
5. Is this an interesting book? — ....
6. Did you have a tiring trip? — ....
7. Do you think she's an appealing child? — ....
8. Do you think he gave a convincing argument? — ....
9. Did you have a frightening experience? — ....
10. Do you think that's an annoying sound? — ....

58 PARTICIPLES AS NOUN MODIFIERS: -ed FORM

Extra Drill 58.1   *-ed* Participle as Noun Modifier

Form noun phrases as in the examples. Use *a* with singular count nouns; use no article with mass nouns and plural nouns.

	TEACHER	STUDENT
1.	The door was closed.	a closed door
2.	The work was finished.	finished work
3.	The story was continued.	....
4.	The man was forgotten.	....
5.	The guests were invited.	....
6.	The facts were known.	....
7.	The watch was broken.	....
8.	The experiment was controlled.	....
9.	The author was celebrated.	....
10.	The onions were boiled.	....

Extra Drill 58.2   *-ed* Participle as Noun Modifier

Complete the sentence with a noun phrase. Study the examples.

1. His *coat* is *torn*.
   He took his *torn coat* to the tailors.
2. His *watch* is *broken*.
   He took his *broken watch* to the jeweler's.
3. The *book* is *illustrated*.
   He bought the .... as a gift for his wife.
4. The *experiment* is *controlled*.
   The government asked him to make a ....
5. The *car* is *stolen*.
   A policeman found the ....
6. The *potatoes* are *baked*.
   Everyone ate a ....
7. A *crime* was *attempted*.
   We reported the ....

8. The *entrance* is *hidden*.
   We finally found the ....

9. Her *effort* is *wasted*.
   She felt all her work was ....

Extra Drill 58.3 — -ed Participle Phrase as Modifier of Noun

A. Form noun phrases. Study the examples.

	TEACHER	STUDENT
1.	A bridge was built in 1632.	a bridge built in 1632
2.	The man was described in the book.	the man described in the book.
3.	The dialog was practiced in class.	....
4.	The exam was given by his math teacher.	....
5.	A package was mailed from Hongkong.	....
6.	One of the men was introduced to us.	....
7.	A house was built by his grandfather.	....
8.	One of the men was selected by the president.	....
9.	A company was formed in 1870.	....
10.	The talk on anthropology was given by Dr. Shook.	....

B. Now listen to the sentence containing the above phrases. Repeat and underline the noun phrases.

1. We crossed *a bridge built in 1632*.
2. We were sure he was the man described in the book.
3. We memorized the dialog practiced in class.
4. The exam given by his math teacher was extremely difficult.
5. I received a package mailed from Hongkong.
6. I already knew one of the men introduced to us.
7. He lives in a house built by his grandfather.
8. One of the men selected by the president was my father.
9. I work for a company formed in 1870.
10. Everyone enjoyed the talk on anthropology given by Dr. Shook.

Extra Drill 58.4 **-ed Participle Phrase as Modifier of Noun**

Combine two sentences into one sentence.
1. Some cars were parked in front of the entrance. They put tickets on them.
    They put tickets on the cars parked in front of the entrance.
2. Many cans are labeled wrong. I'll send them back.
    I'll send back the cans labeled wrong.
3. Some eggs were broken by the children. We had to throw them away.
    ....
4. Some sugar was spilled on the floor. She wiped it up
    ....
5. Many important discoveries were made in ancient times. I'm making a list of them.
    ....
6. Some words are spelled with two *s*'s. I always have trouble with them.
    ....
7. Several cities were suggested as the place for next year's meeting. Chicago was one of them.
    ....
8. Some milk was left in the bowl. The cat drank it up.
    ....
9. Some of the books are published in Canada. There's a higher tax on them.
    ....
10. Several states are affected by tropical storms every year. I don't live in any of them.
    ....

Extra Drill 58.5 **Negative -ed Participle Phrase as Modifier of Noun**

Make the modifiers negative. Study the examples.

1. a question discussed in the meeting   a question not discussed in the meeting
2. the harvested crops   the crops not harvested
3. needed money   money not needed
4. a matter considered by everyone   ....
5. wasted time   ....
6. countries represented at the meeting   ....

7. the dresses sold by the store ....
8. plowed land ....
9. borrowed money ....
10. an answer received by Monday ....

| Extra Drill 58.6 | *-ed* **Participles and Participle Phrases as Noun Modifiers** |

Form participle phrases as in the examples.

TEACHER	STUDENT
1. the papers which were stolen	the stolen papers
2. the chairs which were arranged in a circle	the chairs arranged in a circle
3. the food which wasn't used	the food not used
4. the crops which were produced on that farm	....
5. children who aren't accompanied by their parents	....
6. the answer which is expected	....
7. movies which were produced in Japan	....
8. children who were not raised on a farm	....
9. the country which was divided	....
10. one of the few countries which wasn't represented	....

| Extra Drill 58.7 | *-ed* **Participle as Noun Modifier** |

Speaker A asks the questions. Speaker B gives a short answer based on the statement of fact.

STATEMENT OF FACT
1. The stolen papers were never returned.
2. In her classroom we always sit on chairs arranged in a circle.
3. She put all the food not used back in to the refrigerator.
4. Children not accompanied by their parents will not be admitted to the theater.
5. Children don't always respond with the expected answer.
6. I've always enjoyed the excellent movies produced in Japan.
7. Children not raised on a farm often know very little about animals.

SPEAKER A	SPEAKER B
1. What were never returned?	The stolen papers.
2. Where do we always sit in her classroom?	....
3. What ....?	....
4. Who ....?	....
5. What ....?	....
6. What ....?	....
7. What kind of children ....?	....

Extra Drill 58.8   *-ed* **Participle as Noun Modifier**

Speaker A asks the questions. Speaker B responds as in the models, beginning the reply with "There were..."

STATEMENT OF FACT

1. Three facts were known.
2. Five children were lost.
3. Two people were very worried.
4. 50,000 people were disappointed.
5. Two mirrors were broken.
6. Six cars were stolen.
7. Fifty guests were invited.
8. Eight boys and girls were very tired.
9. Two subjects were required.
10. Four reports were written.

SPEAKER A	SPEAKER B
1. How many facts were known?	There were three known facts.
2. How many children were lost?	There were five lost children.
3. How many people were very worried?	....
4. How many people were disappointed?	....
5. How many mirrors were broken?	....
6. ....?	....
7. ....?	....
8. ....?	....
9. ....?	....
10. ....?	....

59 CONTRAST OF -ing AND -ed FORMS

Extra Drill 59.1 **Contrast of -ing and -ed Participle Modifiers**

Answer the questions as in the models.

1. The story amused him.

    Who was amused?   Hé was.

    What was amusing?   The stóry was.

2. The program bored her.

    What was boring?   The prógram was.

    Who was bored?   Shé was.

3. The trip tired them.
   What was tiring?   ....

4. The speech disappointed the crowd.
   Who was disappointed?   ....
   What was disappointing?   ....

5. The meal satisfied them.
   What was satisfying?   ....

6. The discovery amazed everyone.
   Who was amazed?   ....
   What was amazing?   ....

7. The condition of the world troubled them.
   Who was troubled?   ....
   What was troubling?   ....

8. The idea excited us.
   What was exciting?   ....

9. The class interested her.
   Who was interested?   ....

10. Her questions annoyed him.
    What was annoying?   ....

11. Her reply astonished him.
    Who was astonished?   ....
    What was astonishing?   ....

12. Their answer puzzled us.
    What was puzzling?   ....

60 VERBS FOLLOWED BY TWO OBJECTS: INDIRECT OBJECT WITH *to*

Extra Drill 60.1   **Indirect Object with *to* (Noun Form)**

Repeat the sentence.

1. I gave the book to my sister.
2. He wrote a letter to the company.
3. He paid the money to the bank.
4. He sold his house to some friends.
5. She read a story to the children.

Extra Drill 60.2   **Indirect Object without a Preposition**

Answer the questions using the cued noun phrase. Follow the models.

1. What did they give him? *(some money)*
   They gave him some money.
2. What did she tell them? *(a story about a frog)*
   She told them a story about a frog.
3. What did they write you? *(a long letter)*
   ....
4. What did he give her? *(some hard candy)*
   ....
5. What did she mail him? *(a package of toys)*
   ....
6. What did he show you? *(his chemistry report)*
   ....
7. What did you lend him? *(my English-Arabic dictionary)*
   ....
8. What did he send them? *(a hunting knife)*
   ....

| Extra Drill 60.3 | **Indirect Object with *to* (Pronoun Form)** |

Answer the questions using the cued noun phrase.

1. What did they give him? *(some money)*
   They gave some money to him.

2. What did she tell them? *(a funny story)*
   She told a funny story to them.

3. What did they write you? *(all the news)*
   ....

4. What did he give her? *(some hard candy)*
   ....

5. What did she mail him? *(a package)*
   ....

6. What did he show you? *(his report)*
   ....

7. What did you lend him? *(my new dictionary)*
   ....

8. What did he send them? *(a hunting knife)*
   ....

| Extra Drill 60.4 | **Pronoun Forms of Both Direct and Indirect Objects** |

Change the sentences using a pronoun direct object + *to* + indirect object pronoun.

1. Write him a letter.   Write one to him.
2. Bring me those potatoes.   Bring them to me.
3. Give her a ring.   ....
4. Lend me your notes.   ....
5. Take her the flowers.   ....
6. Sell them a bottle of milk.   ....
7. Read them a story.   ....
8. Offer him your car.   ....
9. Mail her a postcard.   ....
10. Send us our results.   ....

| Extra Drill 60.5 | **Pronoun Form of Indirect Object (with Stress Contrast)** |

Take the part of Speaker A or Speaker B. Study the examples and listen carefully to the stress and intonation of the model sentences. Notice the rise at the end of Speaker A's first sentence.

1. He didn't give the money to me. *(her)*

   SPEAKER A   He didn't give the money to me.

   SPEAKER B   Who did he give it to?

   SPEAKER A   He gave it to her.

2. He didn't show the book to Kim. *(Bill)*

   SPEAKER A   He didn't show the book to Kim.

   SPEAKER B   Who did he show it to?

   SPEAKER A   He showed it to Bill.

3. I didn't lend it to you. *(John)*
4. He didn't send the package to me. *(you)*
5. He didn't write the letter to Joan. *(Pat)*
6. They didn't offer the money to him. *(his brother)*
7. He didn't take the flowers to Mary. *(Jane)*

| Extra Drill 60.6 | **Pronoun Form of Indirect Object (Stress Contrast on Sentence Subject)** |

Take the part of Speaker A or Speaker B. Speaker A makes a statement and Speaker B responds in terms of the statement of fact. Use *one* or *some* for the direct object (Speaker B).

> **STATEMENT OF FACT**
>
> 1. John and Tom both sent Mary some candy.
> 2. He and I both wrote Helen a letter.
> 3. Both the teacher and the librarian told the children a story.
> 4. Both Janet's mother and I lent her some money.
> 5. George and Bob both brought Barbara some flowers.
> 6. Both Lydia and Sylvia gave Joan a gift.
> 7. Mary and John both took their mother some fruit.

SPEAKER A	SPEAKER B
1. John sent Mary some cándy.	Tóm sent her some, tóo.
2. He wrote Helen a letter.	Í wrote her one, tóo.
3.	....
4.	....
5.	....
6.	....
7.	....

Extra Drill 60.7 — **Pronoun Form of Indirect Object (with Stress Contrast)**

Take the part of Speaker B. Follow the models.

SPEAKER A	SPEAKER B
1. John gave me a gíft.	He gave one to mé, tóo.
2. Helen sent me a páckage.	She sent one to mé, too.
3. Mr. Jones wrote me a létter.	....
4. Tom gave me his phóne number.	....
5. Mary brought me some cóffee.	....
6. Dick wrote me a long létter.	....
7. Mrs. Black sent me some jélly.	....
8. Helen showed me her engágement ring.	....

| Extra Drill 60.8 | **Direct and Indirect Object (without Preposition)** |

Using the cues, Speaker A forms questions; Speaker B replies. Observe the model. Read across.

SPEAKER A SPEAKER B
What did *they* give *Bob*? *They* gave *him a watch.*

		CUES	
1.	they	Bob	a watch
2.	she	her mother	a sewing machine
3.	you	your brother	a toy train
4.	he	his father	an orange tie
5.	you	your friend Tom	a silver pen
6.	they	their son	a bicycle
7.	she	her husband	a pair of slippers
8.	he	his wife	a purse
9.	he	his daughter	a party dress
10.	she	her sister	a book of short stories

61 VERBS FOLLOWED BY TWO OBJECTS: INDIRECT OBJECT WITH *for*

| Extra Drill 61.1 | **Direct and Indirect Object with *for*** |

Using the cues, Speaker A forms questions; Speaker B replies. Observe the model.

SPEAKER A SPEAKER B
Can I *get* something for you? Yes. Please *bring* me *some writing paper.*

	CUES	CUES
1.	get	bring some writing paper
2.	do	call a taxi
3.	order	order a steak and some French fries
4.	get	buy the morning paper
5.	do	call a doctor
6.	make	fix a cup of black coffee
7.	do	get the airport on the phone
8.	fix	make a cheese sandwich

| Extra Drill 61.2 | **Indirect Object with** *for* |

Take the part of Speaker A or Speaker B. Base your sentences on the statement of fact.

> STATEMENT OF FACT
> 1. Mrs. Jones bought her daughter a dress yesterday.
> 2. I found them an apartment this morning.
> 3. Bill's wife got him a new tie last week.
> 4. Joe's wife cooked him his favorite dish last night.
> 5. The store ordered us two chairs two weeks ago.
> 6. Helen's father built her a doll house a few days ago.
> 7. The jeweler made Mary a necklace not long ago.
> 8. My friend got me a job last year.

	SPEAKER A	SPEAKER B
1.	When did Mrs. Jones buy her daughter a dress?	She bought it for her yesterday.
2.	When did you find them an apartment?	I found it for them this morning.
3.	....	....
4.	....	....
5.	....	....
6.	....	....
7.	....	....
8.	....	....

| Extra Drill 61.3 | **Indirect Object with** *to* **and** *for* |

Take the part of Speaker A or Speaker B. Base your sentences on the statement of fact.

> **STATEMENT OF FACT**
> 1. I bought her a dress and a sweater.
> 2. We sold him a house and a car.
> 3. He won't build them a house or a garage.
> 4. He ordered us a hamburger and a bowl of chili.
> 5. She sent her son some cookies and a box of candy.
> 6. She made her daughter a skirt and a blouse.
> 7. She won't cook me lunch or dinner.
> 8. I gave him a dictionary and an encyclopedia.

SPEAKER A	SPEAKER B
1. Did you buy her a dress?	Yes, and I bought her a sweater, too.
2. Did you sell him a house?	Yes, and we sold him a car, too.
3. Will he build them a house?	No, ...
4. Did he order us a hamburger?	....
5.	....
6.	....
7.	....
8.	....

62 VERBS FOLLOWED BY TWO OBJECTS: FIXED ORDER

Extra Drill 62.1 **Indirect Object with** *to* **or** *for*

Repeat the first sentence, and then complete the second sentence using *to* or *for*.

1. I don't understand this problem.
   Please explain it *to* me.

2. I can't find my key.
   Will you open the door *for* me?

3. I don't understand this sentence.
   Can you translate it ...... me?

4. Don't you know Mr. Jones?
   I'll introduce you ...... him.

5. I don't know how to say these words.
   Will you pronounce them ...... me?

6. I don't want to lose my watch.
   Will you keep it ...... me?

7. I think he speaks English.
   Why don't you try speaking some ...... him?

8. My radio is broken.
   Do you think you can fix it ...... me?

9. It's cold in here.
   Will you close the window ...... me?

10. I know Helen very well.
    Please remember me ...... her when you see her.

63 VERBS FOLLOWED BY AN INFINITIVE WITH SUBJECT

Extra Drill 63.1 **Verb Followed by an Infinitive with Subject**

Substitute.

I *advised* him to apply for the job.
  asked
  expected
  told
  wanted
  would like

| Extra Drill 63.2 | **Verb Followed by an Infinitive with Subject** |

Substitute progressively.

	I asked him to come to dinner.
to call me a taxi	....
wanted	....
to go to the mountains with us	....
expected	....
we	....
to call on Monday	....
her	....
them	....
I	....
to come to dinner	I expected them to come to dinner.

| Extra Drill 63.3 | **Verb Followed by an Infinitive with Subject** |

Substitute progressively.

	I asked him to go.
want	I wanted him to go.
to help	....
She	....
Yes/No Question	....
expect	....
tell	....
Affirmative Statement	....
to hurry	....
us	....
to study	....
advise	She advised us to study.

| Extra Drill 63.4 | **Verb Followed by an Infinitive with Subject**

Answer the questions using an infinitive with pronoun subject.

1. Is Mr. Jones going to take the job?
   I don't know. I'd like *him to take* it.

2. Is Miss Smith going with us?
   I don't know. I asked *her to go* yesterday.

3. Has John done his homework?
   I don't know. I asked .... it.

4. Did Tom apply for the job?
   I don't know. I advised .... for it.

5. Why is Betty taking science this year?
   Because the university requires .... it.

6. Are you and Tom going to the movies?
   Yes. The Smiths invited .... with them.

7. Is June going to call tonight?
   Yes. I told .... at 9:00.

8. Is your mother going to stay with you?
   Yes. We'd like .... for a long time.

9. Did you help the doctor?
   Yes. He told me he needed ....

10. Is Mr. White going to get tickets?
    Yes. I asked .... two for you.

| Extra Drill 63.5 | **Verb Followed by Infinitive Particle *to* with Subject**

Speaker B answers the questions using the cue word.

	SPEAKER A	SPEAKER B
1.	Is Mary going? *(ask)*	I'm not sure. I asked her to.
2.	Did Mr. Green buy the house? *(advise)*	I'm not sure. I advised him to.
3.	Did Tom get a haircut? *(order)*	....
4.	Did Helen take the books back to the library? *(tell)*	....
5.	Is Barbara going to the dance? *(would like)*	....
6.	Is your son going to college? *(would like)*	....
7.	Is Helen going to the dance? *(invite)*	....
8.	Did Mr. Black get tickets to the play? *(ask)*	....

| Extra Drill 63.6 | **Verb Followed by a Negative Infinitive with Subject** |

Report the negative imperatives as in the examples.

1. I said, "Don't come, Tom."
   I told Tom not to come.
2. We said, "Don't cry, little boy."
   We told the little boy not to cry.
3. She said, "Don't hurry, Helen."
   ....
4. I said, "Don't run so fast, Bob."
   ....
5. The doctor said "Don't worry, Mr. Green."
   ....
6. The dentist said, "Don't eat so much candy, Barbara."
   ....
7. Mrs. Failor said, "Don't play in the street, children."
   ....
8. The policeman said, "Don't cross in the middle of the block, little girl."
   ....
9. Mrs. Thompson said, "Don't forget to set your alarm clock for 7:00, Betty."
   ....
10. I said, "Don't drive so fast, Ted."
    ....

| Extra Drill 63.7 | **Negative Verb Followed by Infinitive with Subject** |

Make the sentences passive, without agent.

	TEACHER	STUDENT
1.	I didn't ask him to leave.	He wasn't asked to leave.
2.	We didn't invite them to come.	They weren't invited to come.
3.	They didn't order us to leave.	....
4.	We didn't tell her to sign the paper.	....
5.	The general didn't order the men to cross the river.	....

6. We didn't expect her to help. ....
7. His parents didn't permit him to drive the car. ....
8. They didn't require us to work seven days a week. ....

64 VERBS FOLLOWED BY A BASE FORM WITH SUBJECT

Extra Drill 64.1   Verb Followed by a Base Form with Subject

Complete the sentences using a base form with subject. Use pronouns.

1. John's getting ready to *go* to bed.
   His parents make *him go* at 9:00.
2. Mr. Jones is *giving* a talk tonight.
   You can watch .... it on T.V.
3. Bill's learning to *drive*.
   We let .... a little every day.
4. Jean *plays* the piano quite well.
   Her mother makes .... two hours every day.
5. Sometimes Tom *comes in* quite late.
   His mother never fails to hear ....
6. Bob *writes* a lot of compositions.
   His teacher has .... one or two every day.
7. He *plays* tennis very well.
   I've seen .... several times.

Extra Drill 64.2   Verb Followed by a Base Form with Subject

Listen to the sentence and the cue. Then form a sentence as in the models.

TEACHER	STUDENT
1. The baby cried. (hear)	I heard the baby cry.
2. He drove away. (watch)	I watched him drive away.
3. She left. (see)	I saw her leave.
4. The children played ball. (watch)	....
5. He went to work. (see)	....
6. She closed the door. (hear)	....

7. A car stopped. (hear) ....
8. They left the house. (see) ....
9. He got out of bed. (hear) ....
10. Someone ran down the street. (hear) ....
11. They sang for a while. (listen to) ....
12. The car ran over something. (feel) ....

65 VERBS FOLLOWED BY A GERUND WITH SUBJECT

Extra Drill 65.1 — Verb Followed by a Gerund with Subject

Substitute.

I *can't understand* his spending all that money for a car.
   don't mind
   resent
   didn't recommend
   worry about
   don't approve of
   didn't like

Extra Drill 65.2 — Verb Followed by a Gerund with Subject

A. **Substitute.**

   She didn't mind *Mr. Smith* coming without an invitation.
             Bill Jones
             Mary
             him
             her sister
             her parents

B. **Repeat the drill using a possessive form.**

   She didn't mind *Mr. Smith's* coming without an invitation.

| Extra Drill 65.3 | **Verb Followed by a Gerund with Subject** |

Take the part of Speaker B. Answer the questions according to the statement of fact. Use a noun + gerund.

> **STATEMENT OF FACT**
> 1. Her sister receives all the attention.
> 2. Her husband wants to buy a new house.
> 3. His parents are getting a bigger house.
> 4. His sister fell into the lake.
> 5. Helen dances well.
> 6. Her son is failing in school.
> 7. Mr. Cholis calls his wife every day at noon.
> 8. Her husband is getting a better job.

SPEAKER A   SPEAKER B

1. What does Helen resent?   She resents her sister receiving all the attention.
2. What does Mrs. White approve of?   ....
3. What is Tom looking forward to?   ....
4. What is John laughing about?   ....

Now answer the remaining questions with a possessive pronoun + gerund.

5. What do they enjoy?   They enjoy her dancing.
6. What is Mrs. Green concerned about?   ....
7. What does Mrs. Cholis appreciate?   ....
8. What is Mrs. Black happy about?   ....

66 VERBS FOLLOWED BY NP (OBJECT) + NP (COMPLEMENT)

| Extra Drill 66.1 | **Verb Object Followed by a Noun Phrase Complement** |

Substitute the noun phrases.

I've always considered him *an intelligent person.*
                         a very capable worker
                         a very fortunate man
                         a very amusing person
                         an excellent author
                         a brave man
                         a man with unusual ability
                         a productive worker

67 VERBS FOLLOWED BY NP (OBJECT) + ADJECTIVE (COMPLEMENT)

Extra Drill 67.1   **Verb Object Followed by an Adjective Complement**

Substitute progressively.

                 I've always considered her intelligent.
capable
We
too serious
found
amusing
He
never
consider
I
intelligent
always   I've always considered her intelligent.

Extra Drill 67.2   **Verb Object Followed by an Adjective Complement**

Complete the sentences as in the examples. Use pronouns.

1. I was happy.   She made *me happy*.
2. They were amused.   We kept *them amused*.
3. John's intelligent.   I consider ....
4. The house was empty.   We found ....
5. The coffee was strong.   I like ....
6. Her hair is long.   She's wearing ....
7. The men were strong.   We proved ....
8. The water was cold.   We kept ....
9. The meat was well-done.   I prefer ....
10. His car was blue.   He'd painted ....
11. The house was clean.   She likes ....
12. The instructions were useful.   I found ....

13. Her coffee is too strong.   She always makes ......
14. The movie was boring.   I found ....
15. They were quite helpful.   We found ....

68 THE USE OF *for* + AN INFINITIVE WITH SUBJECT

Extra Drill 68.1   **Adjective Followed by an Infinitive with *for* + Subject**

A. Take the part of Speaker B. Begin your response with "Was it hard..." Use pronouns.

	SPEAKER A	SPEAKER B
1.	She told John she was leaving.	Was it hard for her to tell him?
2.	They solved the problem.	....
3.	He left yesterday.	....
4.	She asked her mother.	....
5.	They learned to dance.	....
6.	He got a passport.	....
7.	She told her father.	....
8.	They got a telephone.	....

B. Take the part of Speaker B. Begin each response with "Do you think it is really necessary...?"

1.	She's going to come early.	Do you think it's really necessary for her to come early?
2.	I'm going to make an appointment.	Do you think it's really necessary for you to make one?
3.	He's going to all the meetings.	....
4.	She's going to the doctor.	....
5.	He's locking the door.	....
6.	They're going to New York.	....
7.	I'm going to call a policeman.	....
8.	We're recording the drills.	....

ANSWER KEY

(Extra Drill 2.5)
(3) He wants some soap; he doesn't want a towel. (4) He wants some film; he doesn't want a comb. (5) He wants some bread; he doesn't want a roll. (6) He wants some paper; he doesn't want a pen. (notepaper?) (7) He wants some cheese; he doesn't want an egg. (8) He wants some lettuce; he doesn't want a tomato. (9) He wants some glue; he doesn't want a paperclip. (10) He wants some cement; he doesn't want a shovel

(Extra Drill 2.7)
(2) ...a roll of film and a bar of candy. (3) ...two bottles of aspirin, two heads of lettuce and three ears of corn. (4) ...a jar of honey and a jug of apple cider. (5) ...five gallons of gas and a quart of oil. (6) a piece of chalk and two sheets of typing paper. (7) a piece of cheese, two loaves of bread and two cans of beer.

(Extra Drill 3.1)
(1) enough light...a light; (2) Business...the businesses; (3) enough room...another room; (4) my laundry...the laundry; (5) the paper...paper

(Extra Drill 3.2)
A: (3) ...pie; (4) ...a turkey; (5) ...chicken; (6) ...cake
B: (3) ...new medicine...New Medicines... (4) ...an American soup...American soups... (5) ...an unsweetened juice...Unsweetened juices... (6) ...a Turkish tobacco...Turkish tobaccos...

(Extra Drill 4.3)
A: (3) In the jeweler's window, what is the key chain made of? It's made of silver. (4) In the clothing store window, what sells for $22? The cotton shirt. (5) In the clothing store window, what is the sweater made of? It's made of cashmere. (6) In the jewelry store window, what sells for $185? The necklace (does). (7) In the clothing store window, what are the shoes made of? They're made of leather. (8) In the jewelry store window, what sells for $12? The key chain (does). What's it made of? I's made of silver. (9) In the clothing store window, what sells for $39? The pair of shoes does. (10) In the jewelry store window, what sells for $41? The tie pin.
B: (3) Item 14. *Student A:* How much is the flannel shirt? *Student B:* It's $14. (4) Item 5. *Student A:* How much is the silver ring? *Student B:* It's $30. (5) Item 11. *Student A:* How much is the cotton blouse? *Student B:* It's $22. (6) Item 4. *Student A:* How much is the gold necklace? *Student B:* It's $185. (7) Item 12. *Student A:* How much are the denim pants? *Student B:* They're $18. (8) Item 2. *Student A:* How much is the gold ring? *Student B:* It's $85. (9) Item 8. *Student A:* How much are the silver earrings? *Student B:* They're $21. (10) Item 9. *Student A:* How much is the wool dress? *Student B:* It's $130.

(Extra Drill 6.1)
(1) the...an; (2) A...the; (3) a...the; (4) a...the; (5) the...a; (6) a...the; (7) the...a; (8) a...the; (9) the...a; (10) a...the

(Extra Drill 6.4)
(3) Doesn't he want any carrots? No, he doesn't. (4) Didn't she buy some new clothes? Yes, she did. (5) Don't you have some homework? Yes, I do. (6) Don't you need any help? No, I don't. (7) Weren't there any policemen there? No there weren't. (8) Don't we have any homework? No, we don't. (9) Don't you need some money? Yes, I do. (10) Doesn't he have any friends? No, he doesn't.

(Extra Drill 8.2)
(3) Why don't you go to the bank on the corner? (4) Let's go to the cafeteria in the next block. (5) The chalk in this box is yellow. (6) Will you mail the letters on the table? (7) The cream in that bottle is sour. (8) You can borrow the raincoat in the closet.

(Extra Drill 8.3)
(3A) the woman with long fingernails; (3B) That woman with the long fingernails is an actress. (4A) the man with long hair; (4B) The man with long hair is an artist. (5A) the young woman with a white uniform; (5B) The young woman with a white uniform is a nurse. (6A) the young man without a tie; (6B) The young man without a tie couldn't enter the restaurant. (7A) the tall man with glasses; (7B) The tall man with glasses is a professor. (8A) the young woman with the red purse; (8B) The young woman with the red purse is a French teacher. (9A) the lady with black stockings; (9B) the lady with black stockings isn't very young. (10A) the man with a white helmet; (10B) The man with a white helmet is a policeman.

(Extra Drill 9.2)
(2) He loves her. (3) He was looking for it. (4) He is always breaking them. (5) She made them. (6) It itches her. (7) It spoiled him. (8) They walked all over it. (9) I ride the bus with her. (him); (10) He freed them.

(Extra Drill 12.2)
(4) a lot; (5) those; (6) some; (7) enough; (8) two; (9) Five; (10) this (one); (11) a great deal; (12) Many; (13) Several; (14) a lot; (15) a great deal

(Extra Drill 14.2)
(2) She's wearing a funny little pink hat. (3) I saw a beautiful new red fire engine. (4) She's wearing an interesting little red pin. (5) I caught a strange little blue fish. (6) I took a picture of an interesting old white church. (7) He bought a wonderful new white boat.

(Extra Drill 14.3)
(2) He drives a fast little Italian car. (3) He has an expensive new Japanese camera. (4) He's a famous young Brazilian architect. (5) We saw a very interesting Canadian film.

(Extra Drill 16.2)
(3) others; (4) another; (5) others; (6) another; (7) Others; (8) others; (9) another; (10) another

(Extra Drill 16.3)
(3) The other's; (4) the others; (5) The others; (6) the others; (7) The other's; (8) The other's; (9) The others; (10) The other's

(Extra Drill 17.2)
A: (3) He'll tell someone./I won't tell anyone. (4) She lost something./We didn't lose anything. (5) He's decided something./She hasn't decided anything. (6) They've invited someone./We haven't invited anyone.
B: (3) I won't borrow anything./Ann will borrow nothing either. (4) Karl doesn't believe anyone./We believe no one either. (5) They didn't buy anything./I bought nothing either. (6) Susan couldn't hear anything./Carol could hear nothing either.

(Extra Drill 19.2)
(4) Yes, they both... (5) Yes, they both... (6) Yes, they're all... (7) Yes, they all... (8) Yes, they all... (9) Yes, they both... (10) Yes, they all... (11) Yes, they're all

(Extra Drill 20.3)
(3) one of them; (4) of them; (5) of it; (6) of it; (7) of it; (8) one of them; (9) of it; (10) one of them; (11) of them; (12) of it; (13) of them

(Extra Drill 22.1)
(1) ...charming old French restaurant. (2) ...uninteresting white marble statues. (3) ...a talented Brazilian architect. (4) ...ancient Cambodian stone lion. (5) ...valuable oriental brass bell. (6) ...big juicy Florida orange. (6,7) Several small foreign cars....

(Extra Drill 27.1)
(3) ...he was going to the hospital. (4) ...she didn't need anything at the store. (5) ...he thought it was going to rain. (6) ...he believed it was time for him to go. (7) ...he was sure Fred knew the answer. (8) ...she was glad to hear that. (9) ...she thought Doris was going to marry Harry. (10) ...he thought Lydia was in his science class. (11) ...she wasn't sure when she was going to leave. (12) ...he didn't think it was his mistake.

(Extra Drill 27.2)
(3) What did John say?/He said he could speak English and French. (4) What did Helen say?/She said she should study. (5) What did June say to John?/She said she'd teach him how to study. (6) What did Mrs. White say?/She said he had to hurry. (7) What did Bob tell Jim?/He told him he'd like to go. (8) What did Dr. Green say?/He said he had to go to the hospital. (9) What did Mrs. Flower tell Millie?/She told her she'd have to go to bed. (10) What did Jack tell his mother?/He told her he'd help her.

(Extra Drill 27.3)
A: (3) ...he'd like to call her. (4) ...he'd fix the tape for her. (5) ...she should have more patience. (6) ...she could use his book.
B: (2) ...he couldn't take the exam. (3) ...he'd like to go to the Far East. (4) ...I had to practice all the time. (5) ...I had to be on time. (6) ...I'd like the new English teacher.

(Extra Drill 27.4)
(2) ...he'd never studied Spanish. (3) ...she hadn't finished yet. (4) ...she'd never met Doris. (5) ...three students hadn't taken the exam yet. (6) ...she hadn't done the dishes yet. (7) ...he hadn't told anyone. (8) ...all the food had spoiled. (9) ...Tom had gone to school. (10) ...he hadn't eaten lunch.

(Extra Drill 28.1)
These are the questions that the teacher asks.
Teacher: (3) I didn't hear what Tom said. Did you? (4) Can you tell me what Pierre said? (5) I couldn't hear what Mary said. Can you tell me? (6) Did you understand what Roger was saying? (7) I couldn't hear Bob very well. Did you hear what he said? (8) Excuse me. I didn't hear what Mr. Fama said. Can you tell me?

(Extra Drill 28.2)
These are the questions that the teacher asks.
Teacher: (2) I didn't hear Mr. Green. Can you tell me what he said? (3) Did you hear what Mr. Nu said? (4) Miss Foster was talking so low I couldn't hear her. Could you tell me what she said? (5) Excuse me. Can you tell me what Mr. Prado said? (6) Did you hear what Mrs. Blum said? (7) I couldn't hear Mr. and Mrs. Long. Do you know what they said?

(Extra Drill 29.2)
These are the questions that Speaker A asks.
(4) What's Tom writing? (5) Why did he leave? (6) When does the bus leave? (7) Who did you see at the movies? (8) How does he always travel? (9) Who couldn't come? (10) Who did she meet? (11) What did he give her? (12) Why's he sleepy? (13) When will they be back? (14) What did he take to the post office? (15) How do they learn?

(Extra Drill 29.3)
(3) How long is the living room? (4) How wide is Canal Street? (5) How high is that building? (6) How tall is Bob? (7) How long did she live there? (8) How far is it to San Francisco? (9) How often does he play tennis? (10) How much does his brother weigh?

(Extra Drill 30.2)
(3) She asked him how he was going. (4) She asked him whose car he was going in. (5) She asked him what he was going to do. (6) She asked him which movie he was going to see. (7) She asked him what time the movie ended. (8) She asked him what time he would be home.

(Extra Drill 30.3)
(2) Helen asked Jane who she saw at the dance. (3) Bob asked Steve how he broke his watch. (4) Mrs. Jones asked her mother (Mrs. White) when she could visit them. (5) Ted asked June why she was laughing. (6) Tommy asked Billy what he was looking for. (7) Millie asked Irene what they should do. (8) June asked Harriet what she told Tom. (9) Barbara asked Bob when he would teach her how to play tennis. (10) Mr. White asked Mr. Kelly where he worked.

(Extra Drill 30.4)
These are the questions that Speaker A asks.
(2) I couldn't hear Mary./Would you tell me what she asked Ted? (3) Could you hear what Alice said?/Would you tell me, please? (4) Please tell me what Henry said. (5) I couldn't hear George./Do you know what he said? (6) What did Helen say?/Do you know? (7) I couldn't hear./Will you tell me what was said? (8) I didn't hear what Bob said./Did you?

(Extra Drill 31.2)
A: (2) Bob asked Lisa if he could take her picture. (3) Bill asked me if that was my book. (4) I asked Tom if he would call Carlos. (5) We asked Mr. Wilson if he had to leave. (6) I asked if I should go to the meeting.

B: (2) I asked him whether he'd like something to drink. (3) We asked Mother whether she could tell us. (4) I asked Bob whether he knew June. (5) June asked Barbara whether she would call her tomorrow. (6) Mrs. Bell asked her husband whether he was going to apply for the job.

(Extra Drill 31.3)
(2) Tom asked Bob if he'd told anyone. (3) They asked me if Mr. Farmer had arrived yet. (4) Tom asked his brother if he'd decided to go. (5) Mrs. Failor asked me if I'd ever been to Brazil. (6) Bob asked Jim if he'd ever heard of Dr. Ferguson. (7) I asked Tom if he'd seen my history book.

(Extra Drill 31.6)
(9) Are your parents going? (10) Would you like to eat downtown? (11) Does it ever snow in Bolivia? (12) Have you seen that movie? (13) Did Mr. Miles get the job? (14) Mrs. Wilson really wants to go, doesn't she? (15) Is it supposed to rain tomorrow? (16) Would you like to go with us? (17) Did you close the windows? (18) You can go to the movies tomorrow, can't you? (19) Does Bob play tennis? (20) Has Jim left for the Far East yet?

(Extra Drill 33.1)
A: (2) He asked me how my sister was. (3) He told me not to worry about it. (4) He told me my friend was waiting for me. (5) He asked me where I was from. (6) He asked me where I lived.
B: (2) ...she could give us a ride. (3) She asked us where we lived. (4) She asked us (or told us) to put our books in the back seat. (5) She asked us where we learned English. (6) She said (told us) she knew our teacher.

(Extra Drill 33.2)
(3) Lisa asked her if she thought they should go. (4) Bob asked us if we had enough money. (5) I asked them what movie we should go to. (6) Helen asked me if we had a test tomorrow. (7) I said to Helen that I didn't think we did. (8) Jim asked all of us if we should drive or walk. (9) I said to everyone that I thought we should walk. (10) Lisa said to everyone that if we didn't hurry, we'd be late for the movie.

(Extra Drill 34.1)
This is what Mr. Black reported: I said I'd be here from two to four o'clock./He said he'd try to be here at 2:00./I told him Mr. Foster couldn't get here before 2:30./He said he'd see us here at 2:30 sharp.

(Extra Drill 34.2)
(3) He told me he'd seen Tom the day before. (4) He told me he'd be leaving the next day. (5) He told me he'd sent it to me the next day. (6) He told me he'd written to his lawyer the day before. (7) He told me he'd call me the next day. (8) He told me he'd gone to the doctor the week before. (9) He told me he'd pay me the next day. (10) He told me he'd received the letter the week before.

(Extra Drill 34.3)
(1) then; (2) on Monday; (3) that day; (4) the following day; (5) next week; (6) before noon; (7) on Monday; (8) then; (9) the following day

(Edtra Drill 34.4)
These are questions that the teacher asks.
Who's Mr. Watts talking to?/What did he say to her?/What did she reply to Mr. Watts?/Who's greeting the Castles at the door?/What did she say to them?/What did the Castles ask Mrs. Watts?/What did Betty say to Jane?/What did Jane then say to Betty?/Who's Harriet talking to?/What did she ask her?/What reason did Helen give that she couldn't attend the meeting./What is Mrs. Carr asking Dr. Hunter?/What did Dr. Hunter say?

(Extra Drill 36.2)
You're not supposed *to cross the street* here.
                to make a left turn
                to smoke
                to park
                to swim
                to pass
                to speed (or go faster than 35)

(Extra Drill 40.1)
(3) They postponed making... (4) He denies throwing away... (5) He/She advised having it checked... (6) ...includes cleaning... (7) She might risk getting... (8) He used to enjoy walking... (9) We resent having to pay... (10) I admitted leaving...

(Extra Drill 43.2)
(3) Not having it with him... (4) Not putting it in... (5) Not putting them in writing... (6) Not taking it in... (7) Not proofreading them... (8) Not replacing it... (9) Not having it... (10) Not requiring it...

(Extra Drill 46.3)
(3) I'll bring my very warm sleeping bag. (4) They went on quite a long fishing trip. (5) I had to wash all the dirty serving dishes. (6) We have to get rid of our old washing machine. (7) I'm going to have some more of this delicious drinking water. (8) She had to practice the difficult driving lesson again. (9) The house had a huge dining room. (10) Miss Green's getting a green typing table.

(Extra Drill 46.5)
(3) Their seafood is wonderful. (4) The dollhouse was for her birthday. (5) Your notebook's in the car. (6) The sugar bowl's on the top shelf. (7) The orange juice is frozen. (8) Her dessert spoon was under her napkin.

(Extra Drill 46.6)
These are the questions that Speaker A asks.
(5) What did you take on the camping trip? (6) Where can you buy shaving cream? (7) Why are you going to the post office? (8) Do you know where there's a good place to buy some tennis shoes? (9) Where's a good place to buy fresh seafood? (10) How many English teachers are there in your high school. (11) Where can I buy my textbooks?

(Extra Drill 47.7)
(3) Yes, both coffee and tea are popular drinks. (4) Yes, both Tom and Hank want to be engineers. (5) Yes, both Jane and Nancy

hope to be nurses. (6) Yes, both Helen and Barbara are good cooks. (7) Yes, both his wife and (his) daughter are very proud of him. (8) Yes, they had both a radio and a television set. (9) Yes, he speaks both Spanish and Portuguese. (10) Yes, she's both a lawyer and a doctor. (11) Yes, both Dr. Smith and his sister are famous astronomers.

(Extra Drill 50.1)
(3) was; (4) is; (5) is; (6) are; (7) is; (8) lives

(Extra Drill 51.1)
(3) Yes, and the clever are resented too. (4) Yes, and the eternal are hard to define too. (5) Yes, and the sensible make them (mistakes) too. (6) Yes, and the sick were taken care of right away too. (7) Yes, and he can do the impossible too. (8) Yes, and the bad get their names in the newspaper too.

(Extra Drill 52.3)
(3) ...*The Old Man and the Sea,* a famous short story. (4) ...Frank Lloyd Wright, a well-known architect. (5) ...Neil Armstrong, the first man to step on the moon. (6) *A Tale of Two Cities,* a famous novel,... (7) *Fire and Ice,* a well-known poem,... (8) ...Albany, the capital of New York State? (9) ...Echo Lake, one of the most beautiful lakes in the world.

(Extra Drill 53.4)
(3) Yes, I remember having... (4) Yes, I remember eating... (5) Yes, I remember liking... (6) No, I don't remember fighting... (7) Yes, I remember going fishing... (8) No, I don't remember breaking... (9) Yes, I remember playing... (10) No, I don't remember drinking... (11) Yes, I remember going shopping... (12) Yes, I remember sitting...

(Extra Drill 54.2)
(3) It was a three-hour test. (4) It was a two-day job. (5) It's twenty-four floor office building. (6) It's a four hundred seventy-five page book. (7) It was a two-hour lecture. (8) It was a three-month war.

(Extra Drill 53.3)
(3) ...work to do... (4) ...reports to write... (5) ...important telephone call to make... (6) ...letters to type... (7) ...important speech to give... (8) ...patients to see...

(Extra Drill 56.5)
(3) a burning building; (4) a beginning student; (5) students beginning this year; (6) students failing in geography; (7) a developing country; (8) ice melting in the street; (9) melting snow; (10) the amusing girl; (11) the girl amusing her friends; (12) the army attacking us; (13) the attacking army; (14) the boys arguing outside; (15) the men running in the streets

(Extra Drill 56.6)
(3) a continuing problem; (4) the lesson following this one; (5) a pronouncing dictionary; (6) a protecting wall; (7) a paying customer; (8) a thinking person; (9) migrating birds; (10) a sliding glass door

(Extra Drill 58.1)
(3) a continued story; (4) a forgotten man; (5) invited guests; (6) known facts; (7) a broken watch; (8) a controlled experiment; (9) a celebrated author; (10) boiled onions

(Extra Drill 58.2)
(3) illustrated book; (4) controlled experiment; (5) stolen car; (6) baked potato; (7) attempted crime; (8) hidden entrance; (9) wasted effort

(Extra Drill 58.4)
(3) We had to throw away the eggs broken by the children. (4) She wiped up the sugar spilled on the floor. (5) I'm making a list of (the many) important discoveries made in ancient times. (6) I always have trouble with words spelled with two s's. (7) Chicago was one of the (several) cities suggested as the place for next year's meeting. (8) The cat drank up the milk left in the bowl. (9) There's a higher tax on books published in Canada. (10) I don't live in any of the states affected by tropical storms every year.

(Extra Drill 58.6)
(4) the crops produced on that farm; (5) children not accompanied by their parents; (6) the expected answer; (7) movies produced in Japan; (8) children not raised on a farm; (9) the divided country; (10) one of the few countries not represented

(Extra Drill 58.7)
(3A) What did she put back into the refrigerator? (3B) All the food not used. (4A) Who will not be admitted to the theater? (4B) Children not accompanied by their parents. (5A) What don't children always respond with? (5B) The expected answer. (6A) What have you always enjoyed? (6B) The excellent movies produced in Japan. (7A) What kind of children often know very little about animals? (7B) Children not raised on a farm.

(Extra Drill 58.8)
(3B) There were two very worried people. (4B) There were 50,000 disappointed people. (5B) There were two broken mirrors. (6A) How many cars were stolen? (6B) There were six stolen cars. (7A) How many guests were invited? (7B) There were fifty invited guests. (8A) How many boys and girls were very tired? (8B) There were eight very tired boys and girls. (9A) How many subjects were required? (9B) There were two required subjects. (10A) How many reports were written? (10B) There were four written reports.

(Extra Drill 60.6)
3. Speaker A: The teacher told the children a story.
   Speaker B: The librarian told them one, too.
4. Speaker A: Janet's mother lent her some money.
   Speaker B: I lent her some, too.
5. Speaker A: George brought Barbara some flowers.
   Speaker B: Bob brought her some, too.
6. Speaker A: Lydia gave Joan a gift.
   Speaker B: Sylvia gave her one, too.
7. Speaker A: Mary took her mother some fruit.
   Speaker B: John took her some, too.

(Extra Drill 62.1)
(3) for; (4) to; (5) for; (6) for; (7) to; (8) for; (9) for; (10) to

(Extra Drill 63.4)
(3) him to do; (4) him to apply; (5) her to take; (6) us to go; (7) her to call; (8) her to stay; (9) me to help; (10) him to get

(Extra Drill 63.7)
(3) We weren't ordered to leave. (4) She wasn't told to sign the paper. (5) The men weren't ordered to cross the river. (6) She wasn't expected to help. (7) He wasn't permitted to drive the car. (8) We weren't required to work seven days a week.

(Extra Drill 64.1)
(2) him give; (3) him drive; (4) her play; (5) him come in; (6) him write; (7) him play

(Extra Drill 65.3)
(2) She approves of her husband wanting to buy a new house. (3) He's looking forward to his parents getting a bigger house. (4) He's laughing about his sister falling into the lake. (6) She's concerned about her son's failing in school. (7) She appreciates her husband's calling every day at noon. (8) She's happy about her husband's getting a better job.

(Extra Drill 67.2)
(3) him intelligent; (4) it empty; (5) it strong; (6) it long; (7) them strong; (8) it cold; (9) it well-done; (10) it blue; (11) it clean; (12) them useful; (13) it too strong; (14) it boring; (15) them helpful